carbon
detox

detox carbon

Your step-by-step guide to getting real about climate change

george marshall

GAIA
THINKING

*To my lipsmackinwormmulchinquiltdarnin-
darnfastthinkinhotcookinalwayschallengin
alwayslovin wife Annie and in memory of my
dear colleague and friend, Richard Sexton.*

An Hachette Livre UK Company

First published in Great Britain in 2007 by
Gaia, a division of Octopus Publishing Group Ltd
2–4 Heron Quays, London E14 4JP
www.octopusbooks.co.uk

ISBN 978-1-85675-288-6

A CIP catalogue record for this book is available from the
British Library

Printed and bound in Italy

Printed on Cyclus Offset, a 100 per cent recycled paper

2 4 6 8 10 9 7 5 3 1

Executive Editor: Sandra Rigby
Managing Editor: Clare Churly
or: Joanna MacGregor
ester Typesetting Group Ltd
oller: Simone Nauerth

Contents

Part 1
Fresh ways to think about climate change

Chapter 1

Oh, not another bloody polar bear!

Why we need another book on climate change

I have to make a confession. When I hear people talk about climate change I often find myself alternating between despair and boredom.

It's a hugely important and serious issue, and yet most of what I see in the newspapers, in scientific presentations and in the information leaflets of government or green groups leaves me unmoved and unmotivated. I have dedicated my life to this issue, but only because I have worked hard to use my own imagination and create my own storyline. And if the standard communication leaves *me* cold, it can't be doing much for anyone else.

It is this frustration that has led me to write this book. Surely, given the scale and importance of climate change, we can find smarter ways to think and imagine what it means and what it can do

Baffling, boring and irrelevant

A few years ago I attended a scientific presentation to Birmingham City councillors on the impacts of climate change. It was a wonderful opportunity to engage and capture the imagination of decision-makers in Britain's second largest city – an opportunity that was utterly wasted. It was a computer-generated PowerPoint presentation and, as I have come to realize, PowerPoint presentations are rarely powerful or make much of a point.

So we sat through half an hour of charts that showed the parts per million accumulations of obscure atmospheric trace gases and graphs that demonstrated the year-on-year changes in 'precipitation' and the changes in the 'diurnal temperature range' (in normal English that means 'rainfall' and 'difference between night and day'). You can imagine how effective this abstract technical talk was with the practical-minded Brummie councillors. What they needed to know was what it all *meant*: how much would it cost, what would flood, who would die? And even though they never admitted it, I believe they also needed to know how it would *feel* – what would the city that they (and possibly they alone*) love so much look and feel like in the future.

The news media, which makes its living from communicating meaning, has been all over the map. Newspapers oscillate incoherently from hysterical pronouncements of global collapse to hysterical pronouncements that climate change is a leftist conspiracy to destroy people's standard of living. For many years the television news has run endless variations of the same debate. It is called 'is climate change really happening?' and it pits a precise but cautious scientist

*Just kidding, Brummies. I love your city too.

against an aggressively confident charlatan who will tell any lies for a fee.

Climate change reporting has generated a whole B-roll of visual clichés: sweating penguins, polar bears stranded on icebergs, starving people in Africa, a chunk of ice falling into the sea, smoking steel plants, Los Angeles freeways, shimmering heat over cracked earth, big red suns. 'B-roll', by the way, is TV jargon for generic archive material that is used to pad out lazy journalism. The same shot of Arctic ice falling into the ocean has been used so many times that it will outlive the North Pole.

These images all say the same thing: climate change is caused by something else, happens somewhere else and will affect someone else.

If it's so easy why bother?

Solutions to this vast and serious crisis are often reduced to '20 handy household tips'. We can all do our bit, we are told, so turn off your television standby, boil just enough water for your tea, have a three-minute shower. Worse still, a recent green-living book even calls these steps 'easy peasy' as though speaking to a class of enthusiastic toddlers.

People perceive a major imbalance between the seriousness of the issue and the small, 'easy peasy' personal actions they are encouraged to take. As we discover in this book, people always seek to resolve imbalances between what they believe and change what they believe instead – for example, by believing that the problem is less important or finding reasons why there is no point in changing.

So this book does what it says on the cover: attempts to find fresh ways of coming to terms with climate change. I have tried to find new and original metaphors, images and arguments. I hope that you like them and agree, but I am not unduly concerned if you do not. I will be content if they do nothing more than stimulate or provoke you to create your own way of thinking.

Chapter 2

Words fail me

Why we need to find new words for climate change

Throughout this book I talk about 'climate change' but I do so with great reluctance. This is not a phrase that I think measures up in any way to the scale or severity of this issue.

Names – titles – are important: they sum up precisely what we are going to learn about a subject. When we face the most incredible experience in human history, a permanent and destructive transformation in the world's weather patterns, we need a term for it that adequately conveys its significance, power and danger.

All the words we use for it completely fail

The problem with 'climate change'

This is the preferred term of scientists and politicians. Not only does the phrase fail to register the scale and threat of the problem, but it triggers a range of positive and quite inappropriate responses. Take the word 'change' for example. A *change* sounds like something quite gradual, slow, even pleasant. After all, we say, how bad can something be that is 'as good as a rest'.

And then there is that word 'climate'. What is 'climate'? It's not something that we ever have anything to do with. It's the domain of experts – the atmospheric physicists, the climatologists and the meteorologists. Climate describes a large global system that is outside our control, like money supply or ocean currents or trade flows. We may *know* that these things are important, but they *feel* remote and not particularly of immediate concern.

What we actually deal with in our lives is *weather*: the day-to-day fluctuations of temperature and rain that have a direct affect on the areas in which we live. Even then we spend very little of our time actually experiencing the weather. Ninety per cent of an average day is spent indoors.

All in all, the associations triggered by the words 'climate' and 'change' are of a gradual improvement in a remote system of little concern to our day-to-day lives.

So what about 'global warming'?

This back-up term, still commonly used by the public and the media, also completely fails to convey the issue adequately. Scientists argue that talking of 'warming' misrepresents the science. Computer models show that local effects may vary greatly. Although there may be an *overall* increase in temperatures, the shift in climate patterns may make some places far cooler. The phrase is a gift to sceptics, who can point to any extreme cold snap and say 'not much global warming there, ho ho'.

However, the real problem with the term global warming lies with the associations it generates. 'Global' is a word like 'climate' – distant and divorced from our reality. The globe is something seen from outer space, not on ground level.

And *warming* is another word that suggests gradual and positive change. Surely 'warm' weather is the optimum condition for people from any culture. To my mind 'warm' means that we can run around outdoors wearing shorts. The adjective 'warm' has particularly strong connotations in Britain, where the weather is remarkably grey and cool. In the 2003 heatwave, during which summer temperatures reached the highest levels in at least 5,000 years, all of the news reports carried interviews with people on the street saying that it was 'lovely and warm'. For the Brits, 'lovely' is as innocuous a partner for 'warm' as 'nice' is for 'a cup of tea'.

I have thought long and hard about using a different term for the problems we face. Campaigners who want us to redress our negative attitudes often try to introduce new terminology in the hope that it will encourage more positive associations. We now talk of gays not homosexuals, gaming not gambling, sex workers not prostitutes, differently abled not disabled, seniors not elderly. But when I try to find alternative words they sound confusing and laboured – weather change? climate chaos? carbon crisis?

So, with reluctance, I continue to use the term 'climate change' to describe the problem. What I try to do in this book, however, is to redefine that term and encourage you to think differently. Think of climate as weather. Think of a global issue as a local issue. A rest might be a lot better than a change. Warming is the first stage of boiling. My aim is to shift the focus from a change in the climate to a change in our own ways of living and being.

Chapter 3

The Medusa effect

Why a little knowledge is a good thing

I am not going to tell you much about climate change – what it is or what it will do. I will give you just enough information to feel that it is important and that you want to do something. But no more.

Be honest. How do you feel when you hear about the impacts of climate change? When you see a newspaper headline that says 'it's worse than we thought' or 'on the brink' do you feel energized to find out more, or do you feel a strong desire to ignore it or hide?

It has taken me seven years to learn that it is very hard to look directly at climate change without turning to stone. I've given hundreds of public presentations, and for years I made the same mistake – piling on the doom and gloom and forgetting to talk about the opportunities for positive change. People started alert and interested in hearing what I had to say, but little by little I would feel the room chilling. After a few curt questions people thank me coldly and go home, never to be heard from again. I call it the 'Medusa effect'.

A quick historical aside

In Greek mythology Medusa was a beautiful woman, cursed with having a head of snakes and a face that would turn anyone who looked at it to stone. Perseus was sent to kill her by King Polydectes, who wanted to get him out of way so that he could seduce his mother. Perseus managed to kill Medusa by looking only at her reflection in his mirrored shield. He then had lots more fun with the severed head – turning Atlas into a mountain chain and calcifying the lecherous King Polydectes. His life ended in grief after killing his grandfather with a quoit – a murder weapon that never quite made it onto the Cluedo board.

For twenty years campaigners of all persuasions – greens, scientists or government information departments – have been making the same mistake over and over. We are frustrated that people are not moving fast enough. We assume that this is because they don't realize how serious it is, and so we keep piling on the information, grabbing people by the lapels and screaming at them. It's bad – no it's *really* bad – you have no idea *how bad it is*!

Only now are we learning, slowly, how easy it is to push people into a state of despair or self-protective denial – that stony Medusa effect. The best way for people to approach climate change is from behind a reflective shield. They don't need to see the whole thing – they need simply to see how it reflects on their own lives, hopes and dreams. They need just enough information to accept that climate change is serious and concerns them and no more.

So this book is not 'everything there *is* to know about climate change'. It is 'everything you *need* to know about climate change'.

I have picked out a few key ideas and facts, while the Appendices contain details of books and websites aplenty that can tell you everything you *want* to know – *if* you want to.

Chapter 4

The only thing that counts is the carbon bottom line

Why climate change is the only important issue that can be measured

In this book I want you to think about your contribution to climate change as weight, as something that can be measured precisely and down to the last gram. And I want you to think about losing some of it. You can shift it around from one activity to another and choose which bit you want to drop first, but your objective must be to drop as much of it as you can.

You can consider your results and make direct and completely valid comparisons. You can say, 'this year I made half the contribution to climate change that I made last year'. You can say, 'my friends are still far behind me in reducing their impacts' and ultimately, if you go far enough, you can say with confidence: 'I am making no contribution to climate change whatsoever.'

No other problem can be measured in this way. You could never measure your personal contribution to the torture of political prisoners, crack cocaine addiction in the inner city, land mines in Cambodia, stockpiles of nuclear weapons or the deforestation of the Amazon rainforest. We live in a complex and highly interlinked world, so there is certainly some way that you contribute to all of these issues – if not through your personal action then through your votes, your investments, the things you buy, the newspaper you read and so on. But you can't measure it. You may feel strongly about these issues and do everything you can to express your concern. You might protest, lobby and cajole. But you will never know precisely how you are implicated or which of the actions you take are most effective. And you will never be able to say with confidence: 'I am free of any involvement.'

The carbon bottom line

Climate change is different because it can be measured with great precision. As we shall see, climate change is caused by our emissions of carbon dioxide (and a few other greenhouse gases).

→ Up the lift hill (pages 62–7)

The amount we emit can, in theory, be measured down to the last gram. So someone who produces 20 tonnes of carbon dioxide in a year is making twice the contribution to climate change as someone producing 10 tonnes. If you can drop 2 tonnes you are being twice as effective as dropping

1 tonne. Taken together your total emissions of greenhouse gases equal your total contribution to climate change – what I will call your 'carbon bottom line'.

→ Counting the carbos: your total (page 227)

Just because climate change can be measured in this way does not mean that it does not have a moral dimension. Climate change will destroy people's land and livelihoods. Hundreds of millions of people will become environmental refugees. Millions of people will die from weather disasters, floods and famine. In a hundred years' time we will be able to assess the human impacts and weigh them up against the emissions. We may even be able to estimate how many tonnes of carbon dioxide emitted in 2007 led to a death. We don't yet know what that conversion rate is, but we know that there is one (see opposite).

We are used to the idea that we can judge whether something we did was good or bad by looking at our intentions when we did it. But climate change requires you to think quite differently. It makes no difference to the climate whether your flight to Australia is for a party, a holiday, a friend's wedding or to sit by your sister's deathbed. The carbon bottom line, and therefore the real human impacts, will be the same in every case.

This book is based on the concept of quantifying your contribution to climate change and finding that carbon bottom line. How you wish to respond to that information is entirely a matter of your choices, options and the subsequent strategy you choose to adopt.

The emissions–death ratio

Because there is a direct relation between emissions and impacts it should be possible to predict how many people will die for each additional tonne of carbon dioxide we emit – but no academic has yet been bold enough to do it. The variables are huge, especially given the impossibility of accurately predicting how people will actually respond and adapt to the impacts of climate change.

One person who understands the need for this calculation is Craig Simmons. Craig is co-founder of Britain's leading sustain-ability consultancy, Best Foot Forward, and has led major studies into the footprint of London, Scotland and Wales and the 2012 Olympics. Craig reviewed official estimates of the number of people killed and chronically affected by climate-related disasters and combined this with data on global carbon dioxide emissions. His conclusion was that one person could die, be made homeless, require urgent medical treatment or face starvation for every 102 tonnes of carbon dioxide we add to the air.

The average Briton takes nine years to emit 102 tonnes of carbon dioxide, but someone with a flying habit could easily tot it up much faster. A quick scan of the flight calculator on page 207 will show you that 102 tonnes is a lot less than ten return flights to Australia. I have a friend who flies his family once a year to Australia to visit his dad. By this reckoning every 30 months their loving visits wreck someone's life. Or look at it another way: if we don't change the way we live, every person born today who is allowed a high-carbon lifestyle will – over their lifetime – cause the severe suffering of ten others around the world.

Craig would admit that his figures are highly speculative. The causal relationship between emissions and impacts is far from clear. Many disasters go unreported, and the exact mechanisms by which emissions contribute to the undoubted rise in climate-related catastrophes are poorly understood. But they do lead to two very important conclusions: that there *is* a direct ratio between emissions and deaths; and that it is probably low enough for anyone leading a high-carbon lifestyle to be directly responsible for suffering and even death.

Chapter 5

The death of a thousand tips

Why 'small steps' make little difference

In this book I encourage you to abandon the usual messages about the things you can do to prevent climate change. I don't ask you to 'save the planet'. I don't pretend that small, easy steps will 'make a difference'. I want you to be true to what you know and believe and to change the way you think before you change the way you live.

Last month my local council posted a green magazine through my door that asks householders to 'do your bit to save the planet'. It lists a standard set of actions, all of which are phrased as sacrifices – giving things up, doing with less and turning things down – and then assures us that these small personal actions can really 'make a difference'.

Local residents also offered their own tips for low-carbon living. First prize goes to Mrs Roberts who suggests that we turn off the lights when we watch television, as we already have enough light from the TV. Great idea, Mrs Roberts. Sitting in the dark will inspire a lot of people.

And you can find similar things all over the place: on the television, in magazines, brochures and newspapers, and in a plethora of new books full of green lifestyle tips. All of these articles have the same formulae. First, they state that there is a huge global problem. Then they tell people that they have a moral responsibility to take personal actions to stop it. And then they give a list of such actions that are so small and trivial as to appear largely pointless.

I don't doubt the sincerity and good intentions that lie behind them, but I have come to the conclusion that these lists of tips are ineffective and often counterproductive

This is why

First of all, telling people that very small measures can resolve a huge problem is neither honest nor plausible. This trivializes the overall problem and makes us think that maybe it is not such a big deal after all.

The Institute of Public Policy Research (IPPR) argues that these small, trivial measures 'easily lapse into "wallpaper" – the domestic, the routine, the boring, the too-easily understood and ignorable'. The IPPR was especially critical of headlines such as 'Twenty things you can do to save the planet from destruction' and said that putting trivial measures alongside alarmist warnings can lead people to 'deflate, mock and reject the very notion of climate change'.

Second, these lists are misleading because they encourage you to think of different actions as being equally important. A typical list will suggest that you turn off your TV standby and fly less, even though the comparative impact of each is hugely different.

Typical 'tips' with their actual savings

Tip	Kilogrammes of carbon dioxide saved per year
Never use a new plastic bag	5
Change one standard lightbulb to a low-energy lightbulb	17
Never leave your TV on standby	25
Turn down heating by one degree	230 (average house)
Commute to work by bus instead of car	400 (average UK commute in an average car)
Become a vegetarian	500
Make one fewer flight	500–12,000 (depending on the flight)

Clearly there is something very wrong with a list of personal actions that lumps together actions that have a one thousand-fold variation in effectiveness. This is highly misleading and, as we will see later (see The plastic bag fetish, pages 126–8), encourages people to adopt a trivial behaviour change and believe that they are being effective.

Finally, you should not believe that it is *your* responsibility to 'save the planet' or 'stop climate change'. These are slogans to put on banners, not arguments for individual action. Your reasons for changing must be more personal. I want you to change because you decide it is the right thing for you and because you want to do it. Do it because it is the smart 21st-century thing to do. Do it because you don't want to contribute any more to a major problem that will hurt people.

And if you do want to do something, make sure that it is something that actually has results. When facing a serious challenge, 'easy things you can do now' are unlikely to be the most effective solutions. If they were so easy and immediate we would have the problem licked straight away. Everyone contributes in a different way to climate change, and no list of actions will work for everyone.

In this book I treat everyone as an individual and weigh up every action on its own merits. I invite you to seek out your main challenges and then deal with them thoroughly. By the end you will be able to know with confidence how you, personally, can be most effective.

Part 2
Make this book work for you

Chapter 1

Calling real people

Why different people need different messages

Do you ever feel that all that information about green living was written for someone else? Let me describe her (or him – take your pick):

• She is so deeply connected with the world's problems that she only ever does what is right.

• She is so in control of her life choices, and so well organized, that she can immediately stop doing something because it is 'bad', no matter how convenient or fun it might be.

• She never doubts her own judgement and is never confused or distracted by advertising or the views of other people.

• She has enough mental space to take on new and challenging ideas, enough time to implement life changes.

• Last but not least, she always has pots of money to do it all.

OK, you see where I am going with this. I know I'm not describing myself, and I doubt if I am describing you. Actually I've never met anyone like this, and I suspect that if I did, she (or he) would be an unbearable prig without children, a partner or any friends.

Real people are often stressed, short of time and money and struggling with their own insecurities and prejudices. We are driven by all kinds of desires and are pulled about by all kinds of pressures. We rarely respond rapidly to information, no matter how well presented, and are influenced much more by our feelings, aspirations and fears than we would like to admit.

We are all wonderfully, gloriously different, with our own peculiarities, strengths and weaknesses. That is how it should be

So we cannot have a 'one size fits all' approach to a huge and complex challenge like climate change. We need messages that work for us, that recognize that people find it hard to change and that respect all of our differences.

Chapter 2

So who do you think you are?

Why different people are so similar

Here's a paradox: on the one hand we are all different while, on the other hand, we cluster around people who are surprisingly like ourselves.

We strongly prefer to be with people who are like ourselves. Of course we do. I'll bet that your friends and the people around you share most of your interests, tastes, politics and attitudes to life. I'll bet that you eat similar things, watch similar TV programmes and read similar newspapers and magazines. I'll bet that most of the time you could introduce people you like to each other and know that they will get along really well.

So, even allowing for all the huge differences between people in society as a whole, we tend to find that people form distinct groups and that, within these groups, there are many similarities between what people *believe* and what they *do*.

Now, identifying these groups and finding how their attitudes and behaviour combine is very important to retailers, advertisers and politicians; after all, if you can find out why someone buys your product or votes for your party you are halfway to finding the best way to sell it to them. There is a multimillion-pound industry of analysts, marketing theorists and statisticians sending out question-naires, holding focus groups and poring over the sales data so that they can identify those clusters of people who share values, tastes and buying patterns.

Then they name them. They talk about people being 'Seekers', 'Players', 'Optimists', 'Rationals', 'Protectors', 'Flexibles', 'Ethicals', 'Eclectics', 'Transitionals', 'The Tomorrow People', 'The Now People' and so on. They sound like the titles of superhero comic books or those dire 1970s TV action series with two bickering detectives swanning around in a vintage car. *'The President of Moldavia has been kidnapped. If we call the police he will be shot. There are only two people who can deal with this. No one knows their names, but they call themselves. . . "The Transcenders"!'*

Although this comes from the black arts of marketing, these findings have direct relevance to climate change. It is too huge and important simply to assume that everyone has the same response to it or can be spoken to in the same way. If people really do form distinct groups, it has to make sense to address each group separately with different messages about the problem and what they can do about it.

I have waded through the marketing theory and reduced it all down to four basic types of people, whom I have called 'Survivors', 'Traditionalists', 'Winners' and 'Strivers'. Each type has its own concerns about climate change, its own excuses, its own ways of avoiding responsibility and its own potential for positive change.

Although I expect you to identify strongly with one of these types, you will probably be a mix of all four.

Remember that this is a just a handy guide, not a rule book. We are all individuals and rarely fit neatly into a box. Thank heavens.

For example, I tend to be a Striver but my actual life is rife with inconsistencies. However, like everyone, my own life is rife with inconsistencies. I live a low-energy lifestyle but derive much of my personal energy from sausages and pork pies. I am what marketers call an 'early adopter' of new electronic technology but I also love to play 78 records on my wind up Victrola. I favour decentralized communal decision-making but collect Royal Family mugs. If the marketers had ever found anyone else in my attitudinal cluster I think they might call us the Anarcho Fogey Mincetarians. I don't think that we offer much hope for the President of Moldavia, though. We'd probably eat him.

Now it is time to find your own type. Over the next four chapters I will talk about each type. Please read through each one and consider which of these categories works best for you.

Chapter 3

Personality type A
Survivor

Against all the odds, you somehow manage to hold everything together. You feel under pressure from many directions – family, work, health or money – and it is these pressing issues that often control your life. You hope that things will ease up at some time in the future, but for the moment you know that if you deal as best you can with the emergencies as they come up you will get through it all.

Sometimes you feel that you are just about on top of things, and sometimes you feel overwhelmed. Time and money are precious commodities in your life, and when you get hold of either you want to spend it on yourself doing something that helps you to recover.

You and climate change

You already feel that your life is quite full enough with challenges. When you hear about climate change you probably think, 'Oh no, the last thing I need is another problem!' and although you are concerned, you trust that the government will sort it out.

In any case, you are living in the moment and most of the things you hear about climate change seem far away and have little relevance to the day-to-day realities of your life.

You probably feel irritation when people tell you that you should do this or that to 'save the planet', reckoning, with good reason, that they have no idea what it is like to be in your shoes and suspecting that other people could be doing a lot more. 'It's easy for *them* to tell me to drive less,' you think. 'They don't have to drive 20 miles (30 km) to the only job that can pay the rent.'

Often what people say sounds like a fundamental criticism of the way that you live and their solutions involve creating more work for you or taking away something you really value – like the annual family holiday, which is your one chance to unwind.

How this book can help you to think about climate change

Climate change is a reality

Think of climate change as a reality in your own world: something that will affect you, your job and your community. You want stability and security and need to recognize that you can feel secure in the climate-change world only if you are prepared for it. The way that you can put yourself and your family in the best position is to recognize and adapt to the changes that are coming.

→ The climate rollercoaster (pages 59–84)
→ Strategy 2: Adapt (pages 141–9)

You will be all right

Don't think that climate change will destroy your life. It won't, if you are prepared for it. Remember that you are strong and you, of all people, are well prepared to deal with whatever life throws at you.

➔ You *will* be OK (pages 80–1)

A low-carbon society will be good for you too

You will be the main benefactor of many of the measures needed to deal with climate change: they will make life easier for you, reduce your overheads and create local employment. You may even find that you can make money from selling carbon credits to rich people – the first time in human history that people with modest lifestyles will be rewarded.

➔ The vision (pages 152–5)

Do the things that make sense for you

Ignore all of the blather about doing this and doing that. Focus on a few simple measures that will make sense for *you* and will put you in the best position for the future. Insulating your home makes perfect sense. It will save you money and make your home more comfortable.

➔ Drop a tonne at home (pages 238–44)
➔ The DIY weekend to drop a tonne (pages 245–8)
➔ Drop a tonne on home power (pages 249–53)
➔ Blue moon opportunities (pages 279–80)

You are not on your own

Many of the things you can do will not cost you much money or time. There is more and more and more help available for reducing energy use, including information packs, phone lines and government grants. If you are on benefits or a state pension the government will pay all the costs of insulating your home. If you live in rented accommodation there are schemes for landlords, helping them to save on most of the costs – all you need to do is make a few phone calls to get it moving.

→ Appendices (pages 315–37)

Avoid the blame game

You feel under stress, so it is only natural for you to protect yourself by passing the buck and telling yourself that someone else is responsible for the problem. Be aware that, as we get deeper into climate change and people get more scared, they will start looking for someone to blame. There will be plenty of people looking for a chance to stir you up, and these people may create an enemy for you to turn against: another class, another country or refugees fleeing the impacts of climate change – after all, this would not be the first time that the victims are blamed for the problem.

→ Hiding in the crowd (pages 129–31)
→ Meet your Evil Carbon Twin (pages 132–8)

If you prepare yourself for climate change you can survive all of the changes that are coming. The first step is to accept it and start taking simple steps to adapt.

Chapter 4

Personality type B
Traditionalist

You like things the way they are. You are proud of what you have achieved. You have worked hard and saved for the things you have, and you have always been careful to live within your means. You admire people who have made something of their lives providing that they play by the rules.

You love tradition, history and your country. Your life is centred around your home. You are a good neighbour, are involved in local community life and are always polite and law-abiding. You have mixed feelings about the modern world. On the one hand, you believe strongly that you have earned the right to enjoy modern luxuries through your own hard work. On the other hand, you notice the growing rudeness, selfishness and violence of society and fear that new ways of living may make things worse.

Your attitude to change could be summed up as, 'If it ain't broke, don't fix it' although, as a stickler for good English, you would probably prefer 'if it is not broken, then refrain from fixing it'.

You and climate change

You like nature and you have noticed that the weather is changing rapidly. You accept that the scientists are telling us that we have a big problem, but you may suspect that it is exaggerated by other people, who are stirring things up for their own political reasons.

You find the idea that human behaviour can permanently alter the weather deeply unsettling and would prefer to believe that this is just some natural cycle. Traditionalists are particularly susceptible to the arguments of professional climate deniers, especially when they appear to be scientists who speak with authority.

When you hear people talk about the solutions to climate change you suspect that they want to take something away from you. Your immediate reaction is that you will have to defend the things that you have worked for against the people who want to take them away. You suspect that the government is using the issue of climate change as an excuse to increase taxes and that political activists are hopping on the bandwagon because they want to undermine your values and way of life.

Your own frugality and good money sense help you to keep your bills under control, but you may be slow to renovate your house or replace an inefficient old car or appliance when it seems to be 'doing the job'.

'Traditionalists' tend to stay close to home and have holidays in Britain, although it is always possible that you have caught the travel bug. If you do fly, you may well clock up major air miles visiting far-flung family members. Although you would never think of flying to Europe once a month, you could easily burn as much fuel flying to Australia once a year.

How this book can help you to think about climate change

Trust your own eyes

You know from what you can see with your own eyes that climate change is real. The scientists all agree, and those who don't are not to be trusted. You strongly support honesty, so remember: the people who tell you that climate change isn't happening are lying.

→ Stifling your inner sceptic (pages 103–8)
→ Bad messengers (pages 109–15)

Climate change is your issue

This is not an environmentalist issue or another government problem: this is *your* issue. It will affect all the things you care most about: your house, your garden, the countryside and all our history and traditions. If your house is vulnerable to flooding it may well become impossible to sell.

→ Over the top (pages 71–7)

Climate change is not fair

You have an innate sense of 'fair play' so you need to recognize that climate change is not 'fair'. Your lack of action could destroy the future for your children and grandchildren and others all around the world.

→ The only thing that counts is the carbon bottom line (pages 22–5)

Give the government the power to act

If you think that it is the government's job to do something, then demand that they do that job and vote for the parties and candidates who will deliver the most. But recognize that their job will involve telling everyone – including you – what you can and cannot do. Usually you would strongly resist this, but you must recognize that this is one of those rare and urgent issues when we all need to pull together.

→ Rectify (pages 302–4)

We need that Blitz spirit

Remember that the British are a strong and defiant people. In 1939 we pulled together and did everything that was necessary to defeat Nazism. Climate change is a crisis on a similar scale, and we know that we have the guts to pull together and deal with it.

The solutions are things you already support

Many of the solutions to climate change are things that you support and value. Take travel, for example. We will have to stop rushing about so much and focus on our community. We will need to take holidays closer to home – is it such a bad thing to support British holiday resorts and hotels? And what about food? We will have to support our own local farmers and buy local food from local shops instead of flying and trucking food from all around the world. Surely that's something you can support?

→ The vision (pages 152–5)
→ Reason 4: You are already halfway there (page 168)

Thrift is good

People will need to be a bit more thrifty and economical with their energy. You understand what it is like to live within your means. Surely it would be a good thing if people stopped shopping so much and made do with a little less. And, whatever you think of climate change, you know that you can save money and increase the value of your house by making it more energy efficient. In fact, when you look at what you need to do you may find that you are already living a low-carbon life. Would it be a bad thing if other people lived a bit more like you?

By recognizing climate change and acting against it we can become prouder, stronger, more confident and more united. It threatens everything we have achieved and everything we hold dear, so are we going to just sit around or are we going to put up a fight?

Chapter 5
Personality type C
Winner

You are excited by the modern world and everything it offers. You see life as a game that you intend to win, so you look to successful and famous people for your role models – the sportspeople, entrepreneurs and stars who have worked hard and really made it. You enjoy the apparent choice and freedoms of the modern world. You like to own new smart things and to travel. You love shopping, especially for well-known brands that show your success. And, let's face it, you like to live for the moment and are not the world's greatest saver!

You are very sociable and like working and playing in a team rather than on your own. However, because you really don't like to feel too tied to one place or job you move around often, and your friends are likely to be a dispersed network rather than a community.

If you are a Winner you like change. You welcome it into your life and actively seek it out when you feel that you are getting too set in your ways. You tend to be optimistic, reckoning that despite any problems things are on the up and that you have the skills that will enable you to survive any bad times that come along.

You and climate change

You accept that climate change is happening, but you find it hard to accept the scale or urgency of the problem. Your optimistic and positive nature is not receptive to bad news and suspects that it has all been rather exaggerated. You are probably not sympathetic to environmentalists and see them as whingers and killjoys.

Unlike the Survivors and Traditionalists (see pages 37–40 and 41–5), you are not threatened by change. In fact you almost welcome it. You are certainly the type of person who might feel excited by the fantasy that Britain could turn into the Costa del Sol.

You enjoy your lifestyle and aspire to more of the 'good things in life'. You are therefore suspicious of anyone who seems to tell you that you will need to give anything up, especially your mobility, holidays or possessions. You may react strongly against them or brush them off as 'eco-freaks'. As someone who watches carefully to see what other people are doing, you are very likely to say, 'why should I make a sacrifice when no one else is doing anything?'

In truth though, climate change probably doesn't figure much in your life yet. The people around you are not talking about it and so you find it hard to believe that it could be important to you.

How this book can help you to think about climate change

Climate change threatens your success

Sorry to say it, but you are seriously underestimating the extent to which climate change threatens everything you've worked for. There will be major economic costs, and people who work in the wrong businesses or have a house in the wrong place could be ruined.

→ Strategy 2: Adapt (pages 141–9)

Low-carbon living says *great* things about you

You care what people think of you and you like to make a good impression. When you embrace climate change and the detox you are sending out a strong message to the world: 'I am smart, modern and living in the 21st century.'

→ Find a lifestyle that says nice things about you (pages 177–9)

High-carbon lifestyles will go out of fashion

Climate change will lead to huge changes in social attitudes. The things that are currently marks of success will start to be seen as symbols of the problem. People may stop seeing your lifestyle as smart and sexy and start to see it as something sad and ugly. Remember that when people get scared they often look for someone to blame, and you might become a target.

→ Say no to sackcloth (pages 161–3)

Embrace the challenges

There are big changes coming, and people who are smart will be a part of them. They will embrace the 21st century, rebuild their houses, change their lifestyles and get into the new growth areas. It's a challenge, but you respond well to challenges, and this is certainly the path to feeling positive and good about yourself.

➔ The carbon detox (pages 158–60)
➔ You know it makes sense (pages 164–71)

Climate change will create the 21st-century winners

People who are alert to the new opportunities presented by climate change could do very well. After all, once you know about climate change it is like being given an insider tip on the options for the future, and there are fame and fortune for the people who listen to that tip. The people who don't catch on will be left behind in the 20th century, feeling overwhelmed and constantly scrabbling to catch up.

➔ Thriving (pages 283–9)

You can live smarter

It is important that you see climate change as a call to live differently to meet the challenge of exceptional times. There will be some things that you may no longer be able to do, but this does not mean that your life need be less fulfilling – indeed, it may well be happier and richer if you engage with climate change.

➔ Drop a tonne on air travel (pages 265–8)
➔ Drop a tonne on stuff (pages 271–6)

→ The vision (pages 151–5)

Go shopping

Oh, and you know what? There will be lots of smart new things to buy! Having a solar panel, a fuel-efficient car or a zero-energy house will become the mark of a successful person. And you could be the first person you know to have one.

→ Enjoy your treats (pages 172–6)
→ You can buy some great stuff (pages 169–71)

The people who will be respected, admired and successful are those who recognize climate change, abandon 20th-century lifestyles and position themselves to benefit from the new opportunities. So how do you intend to respond to this challenge?

Chapter 6

Personality type D
Striver

Your motto is, 'I want to be better and I want the world to be a better place.' You regularly ask yourself whether your life is contributing to these goals. Your principles are very important to you, and you don't like to compromise them. You are not particularly concerned with money or possessions and choose your work or personal lifestyle on the basis of their ethical value or the personal satisfaction they give you. Many 'Strivers' are more concerned with finding a spiritual dimension to their life through art or religion.

In your personal relationships you seek intimacy and honesty. You are not interested in knowing lots of people if you feel that your dealings with them are superficial or phoney. So you can be content with a small circle of sustaining friends and family, and you may well be self-contained and happy on your own.

You are keenly aware that there are many problems in the world, and sometimes you feel quite pessimistic about the future. You are not afraid to be outspoken about something that you think is wrong: people's opinion of you are less important to you than your sense of what is right and your honesty to yourself.

You like to live simply but also enjoy change if you think it will be a personally enriching experience. You do not feel bound to any one place and see yourself as a global citizen. You are interested in nature and other cultures and enjoy travelling and discovering new things about yourself and the world.

You and climate change

Of all the personality types, you are the most likely to accept climate change and its implications. You are quite able to believe that humans are damaging major environmental systems through selfishness and greed and that they need to change.

This does not mean that you yet accept the full importance or urgency of climate change. After all, you are bound by the same natural denial mechanisms as everyone else, and climate change has to compete for your attention with a lot of other issues. You may well fail to see the connections and see climate change as a lesser problem than poverty, human rights abuses or war.

As an ethically driven person you believe that you have a personal moral responsibility to do something and lead the way. In fact, you probably believe that Britain would be a better place if people made do with fewer things and depended on each other more.

However, because you are not particularly concerned with material things your own emissions can be quite high. You are prepared to put up with a badly insulated old house rather than spend the money to renovate it properly, and you tend to keep old inefficient appliances and cars running to the bitter end. You are particularly prone to making token changes, while missing the really major contributions that you make to the problem.

And, because you are so interested in finding out more about the world, you may well have a weakness for air travel. Some younger Strivers live very simply but spend all their spare money flying to remote places to visit nature or do voluntary work.

How this book can help you to think about climate change

Climate change is a crime

To protect our own wealth and well-being we are destroying the welfare of the world's poorest people. When one group of people forcibly removes something from another group for their own benefit, it is called a crime. And climate change is the greatest crime that we have ever committed because, ultimately, the people we are stealing from are our own children and the world's most vulnerable people.

→ The only thing that counts is the carbon bottom line (pages 22–5)

Climate change will affect every issue you care about

Climate change is not an isolated problem. It will further impoverish the world's poorest people, create new conflicts over water and land and generate millions of environmental refugees. There is no issue of global concern that will not be affected.

→ Over the top (pages 71–7)

The solutions will help in many other ways

Insulating every house in Britain will provide jobs, eliminate fuel poverty and prevent the deaths of thousands of elderly people from cold each year.* Shifting to renewable power will end, once and for all, the environmental devastation and corruption of the fossil-fuel industry. And the imperative of taking action on emissions can create a new era of international cooperation.

→ The vision (pages 151–5)

A low-carbon life is a more fulfilled life

You don't have to be motivated by guilt, however. Consider the reduction of emissions as just another aspect of your lifelong search for a more fulfilled and enlightened life. Don't forget, though, that achieving real change requires that you amplify and multiply with action at both a local and national level. You should start by putting your own life in order, but be careful not to hide your solar-powered light-emitting diode under a bushel. Tell everyone!

→ The carbon detox (pages 158–60)
→ Say no to sackcloth (pages 161–3)

*According to Help The Aged, 20,000 elderly people die each winter from cold, damp and poor housing. This is the highest rate of winter deaths in Europe and it should be a source of national shame.

This is your historic calling

This is the greatest crisis ever faced by humanity and you are prepared to lead the way. Although you don't really believe in 'leaders', you know better than anyone that the actions of a small number of dedicated people have changed the world in the past. The movements that ended slavery, apartheid and colonialism all started with a few people who heard an historic calling. Now an even greater issue is calling you.

➜ Thriving (pages 283–91)
➜ Taking control (pages 293–304)

You need to assess and reduce your own contribution

You need to take responsibility for your emissions. In this case you will not be able to depend on your internal judgement to tell you if you are doing the right thing. You need to do a full carbon audit and change your behaviour accordingly. For example, you probably believe that your air travel is more worthwhile than other people's because you want to learn about a country and its people rather than sit in a resort. But the climate doesn't care why you made the trip: as we found in the last section (pages 22–5), the only thing that counts is the carbon bottom line.

➜ Counting counts (pages 184–7)

Climate change is the greatest moral challenge we have ever faced. We need your vigilance to make sure that we never forget our responsibility to the rest of the world to take real and lasting action.

Chapter 7

Got the message?

Why finding what works for you is the best way forward

So, did you identify with any of the personality types: The struggling Survivor, the thrifty and change-averse Traditionalist, the high-living Winner or the ideological Striver?

I would imagine that you identified closely with one of them, discovered you had components of the others and felt that there were some parts of yourself that were not represented at all. Good – it would be a sad world if we all fitted neatly into marketing definitions.

What I hope you did notice, though, was that the different types respond to climate change in very different ways and need very different messages. The messages that work best for one group would completely fail with another.

Unfortunately, government agencies and green groups keep making the same mistake and using the wrong messages for the people they are talking to. They keep telling Survivors that this is another threat, when they should be reassuring them. They keep telling Traditionalists that they need to make huge changes to save the world, when they should be telling them that there are solutions in the way that they live already. They keep telling Winners that they can save money by insulating their loft, when they should be telling them how they can succeed in a climate-change world. And increasingly they are telling Strivers that they can 'be cool' by buying the latest eco-products, when most Strivers won't be 'cool' until they are six foot under.

The messages are often all wrong. Still, I am sure that you are too smart to ignore climate change just because you don't like the way it is being sold to you

So I suggest you pick carefully through everything that is said, choosing what is useful to you and developing your own arguments and ideas. Climate change is a huge problem and there is an infinite number of ways that we can tackle it. All that is important is that you find the way that works for you. Before you can do that, however, you are really going to have to believe that climate change is happening. In the next two sections we look at the realities of climate change and then at the reasons why we find it hard to accept this problem.

Part 3
The climate rollercoaster

Chapter 1

Roll up, roll up

All aboard for the climate rollercoaster

Roll up! Roll up for the ride of your life! This is going to be an incredible journey – an entirely new experience for humanity.

You'll have to hold on tight because you're really going to feel the G-force on this ride. The little car is going to rocket up and drop like a bomb, spin upside down, hurtle round 180-degree bends, arc and whip to the left and right.

Don't worry, you're not alone. We're all in it together, all strapped down into the same seats. We will all feel the same sense of panic in the pit of our stomachs as we go over the top and relief as we level off. We will share the experience and find joy in the closeness we feel.

We will share the experience with each other. We're going to wave our hands in the air as we go over the top. We're going to scream together as we whip round that 180-degree twist and we'll howl as we tip upside down.

We're going to admit to ourselves – and to others – that we are scared. We will admit that this is one hell of a ride and that, on reflection, we would prefer not to be on it. But we're going to ride it out all the same.

With a positive attitude we can accept this rollercoaster ride and do everything we can to keep our little car on the track. And while it may feel terrifying, we trust that we're going to be OK because we're prepared physically and mentally and know that we can depend on each other's support.

Chapter 2

Up the lift hill

How the sun powers the ride

After years of struggling to understand climate change as an abstract global system, I realized that I could understand it much better if I thought of it as a scary personal journey in which I had little influence – a high-velocity rollercoaster.

Let's be clear, I am no fan of rollercoasters, although it has taken me twenty years to realize that I really *can* be a man without going on them. The last rollercoaster I dared to go on was the notorious Cyclone at New York's Coney Island. When it opened, Charles Lindbergh said it was 'scarier than flying solo across the Atlantic', and that was in 1928, when flying across the Atlantic was a lot more dangerous and the Cyclone still had new bolts. On the back of my ticket was a legal indemnity declaring that I had renounced my right to sue in case of loss of life or limb. It was hardly reassuring that the man who started the ride had only one arm with which to pull the lever.

But in retrospect, the most terrifying part of the Cyclone, or any traditional rollercoaster ride come to that, is the ascent – called the 'lift hill' in coaster parlance. It feels OK to begin with but as you rise higher and higher your misgivings grow. You become increasingly aware of your height and the speed with which you are going to fall. You realize that you are a bundle of potential energy waiting to go kinetic. Then there is a little hiatus at the very top during which everyone, hardened coasties included, wonders quite why they are doing this to themselves.

Climate change is still on its lift hill. We know that things are steadily ratcheting up. There's less snow, there are sudden and extreme downpours and strangely warm winters with daffodils coming up three months early. We hear of typhoons, droughts and fires in other parts of the world.

Our car is getting a little wobbly and a bit higher than we might like, but it doesn't feel too bad yet and there are plenty of distractions as we make our slow but steady ascent. Now I don't want to overstress the comparison between climate change and this rollercoaster. The rollercoaster is a just metaphor, a tool for understanding, not a literal model for how climate change works.

What powers the rollercoaster?

The rollercoaster analogy is quite fair in one important respect: rollercoasters and the global climate are both mechanisms for distributing energy. On a traditional coaster, the speed with which the cars go around the ride is entirely determined by the height of the ramp. That unlikely rollercoaster fan Albert Einstein cited the roller-coaster as a perfect example of energy conservation in a mechanical system, by which he meant: the higher the lift, the greater the potential energy, and the faster and wilder the ride down.

The energy that powers the world's climate systems comes directly from the sun. There are huge differences between the heating of different parts of the world, depending on the seasonal tilt of the earth, the latitude of a given area and whether it is covered by land, sea or ice. The world's climate systems resolve these differences and redistribute that energy through air currents, cloud formations, rain, winds and ocean currents. Like the roller-coaster, if you add more energy at the front end of the system you also strengthen the mechanisms that disperse it.

For over a hundred years we have known that some gases have a special quality: they hold onto some of the energy in the sun's rays and 'trap' that heat in the atmosphere. This has some similarity to the way that glass traps the sun's heat in a greenhouse, and for this reason these gases are called 'greenhouse gases'.

The main greenhouse gases

The 'global warming potential' of gases is measured in terms of carbon dioxide, the main greenhouse gas. Thus, some manmade gases can be thousands of times more powerful than carbon dioxide – fortunately, they are released in relatively low quantities.

Gas	Non-natural cause	Global warming potential
Carbon dioxide	Fossil fuels, deforestation, cement production	1
Methane	Fossil fuels, paddy fields, waste dumps, livestock	21
Nitrous oxides	Fertilizer, industrial processes, fossil fuels	310
Chloro-fluoro carbons (CFCs)	Liquid coolants	1,000–7,000
Sulfur hexafluoride	Electrical switching equipment industry	24,000

Now, over the past 200 years, we have been on a massive burning spree. We started with vast forest clearances in Europe, Australia and the Americas, followed by an industrial revolution fuelled by coal, oil and gas. When we burn these fuels, carbon laid down and permanently locked up 300 million years ago is liberated and re-combines with oxygen to make carbon dioxide.

Over this time we have added a thousand billion tonnes more carbon dioxide to the atmosphere

The air bubbles trapped in Antarctic ice give scientists a very accurate snapshot of previous carbon dioxide levels. In 2006 they drilled 3 kilometres (1.9 miles) into the ice to extract ice that was laid down 800,000 years ago. The air bubbles captured in this ice show that carbon dioxide levels have varied from 180 parts per million during cold periods (there have been eight ice ages during this period) to 300 parts per million during the warmest times. Current levels of carbon dioxide in the atmosphere are 380 parts per million, so we can say with confidence that the current level is the highest in 800,000 years and many scientists believe that it is at its highest level for 20 *million* years.

How greenhouse gases effect the weather

Greenhouse gases trap the heat of the sun and increase the amount of energy that powers the world weather systems. So how much energy is this? A huge amount. The greenhouse gases that we have added to the atmosphere now trap an additional 1,200,000,000,000,000 watts of the incoming solar radiation. This is 120 times the total energy released by the nuclear bomb dropped on Hiroshima. Whereas an atom bomb releases its power in a fraction of a second, the greenhouse gases are adding this amount of energy to the world's climate systems constantly.

This additional energy is putting immense strains on the world's climate systems. The winds that distribute that energy are becoming faster and stronger. The number of Atlantic hurricanes forming each year is now twice as many as in 1900.

Entire climate cycles are becoming shorter and more intense, the El Niño oscillation brings extreme rainfall in South America and drought to Australia and the Pacific. It used to occur once every 10 to 15 years. By the 1980s it was occurring every 3 to 5 years, and in recent years it has accelerated further to every 2 to 3 years.

At some point the existing cycles may prove unable to handle the additional energy, and they could shift to entirely new patterns. Climate scientists argue that sudden changes have occurred frequently in the past. On occasion, entire climatic zones have relocated within just a few decades.

If we think of climate as a closed energy system like a rollercoaster, the additional energy introduced by the increase in greenhouse gases is the equivalent of building that lift hill very high indeed. We are now talking about a very, very high rollercoaster. Never mind the weeny 90 metre (300 foot) Millennium Force in America, which claims to be the 'tallest and fastest rollercoaster on the planet Earth'. Empty bragging. The climate rollercoaster is turbo-powered by 120 atom bombs. There's going to be lot of Gs on this ride and a very high lift hill. And here is the real catch. We are only now feeling the effects of the emissions of our parents. We will not feel the effects of our own emissions for at least 30 years. That is why we are still on the lift hill and the real ride is yet to come.

So far, very few people have cottoned on to what kind of ride awaits us. There are a few people at the front of the car pointing and shouting: 'Look how high this damned thing goes', but few of us are listening. Yes, we know that we are going up, but it still *feels* OK so we are not too worried . . . yet.

Chapter 3

You're already on the rollercoaster

Why you get no choice about this ride

Everything you've heard so far is the sales pitch for the rollercoaster – the roll up, roll up. Maybe you've been looking it over and thinking: 'Well that might be one hell of a ride, but I think I can do without it.' I don't blame you.

The problem is that you don't get the choice. You're already on it.

Accepting this is the first major challenge for people when they hear about climate change and one of the reasons why people are in such denial about it. No one wants to accept the truth – that we are already committed to 30 years of dangerous changes in the world's weather by the greenhouse gases that are *already* in the atmosphere.

Scientists use the word 'commitment' for the extent to which certain major impacts are unavoidable. Science has its own language, but for once this word translates perfectly into normal English. We are on the ride and we are committed to seeing it through.

And it is not as though we haven't been warned. Back in 1965 the President's Science Advisory Committee (PSAC) warned President Johnson that the rapidly increasing levels of carbon dioxide 'will modify the heat balance of the atmosphere to such an extent that marked changes in climate could occur'. Even then we knew we were cranking up that lift hill.

It took another 18 years before 'global warming' received its first mention on British television evening news. I'll bet that you didn't pay much attention to it. Certainly I didn't. Back in 1983 I had my whole life ahead of me. Two years later I was applying for jobs in international finance and flying off around the world.

And here we are another quarter of a century later and we are finally realizing that something is going on. I go out of my house and it feels like a lovely spring morning – it is mild and balmy (not sunny, of course; we're still living in Britain after all). The daffodils are coming up, the birds are singing, the buds on the hedge are forming. Just one problem – it is January 2007, and spring is not supposed to start for another two and a half months.

The winter of 2006–2007 was the warmest across the northern hemisphere since records began, and the changes have been noticeable everywhere.

• In Austria the world downhill ski championships faced cancellation owing to a lack of snow. The organizers had to hire ten helicopters at a cost of $390,000 to fly snow in from higher up the Alps.

• In Moscow zoo the bears suffered months of insomnia before finally hibernating. In Spain bears gave up hibernating altogether.

• In Italy peach, plum and apricot trees blossomed months early as did the famous cherry trees in Japan. And in tropical Swansea a retired couple found a grapefruit fruiting in their garden.

• In Cyprus wild asparagus emerged in late February, two months early. One man was picking it when he was bitten by a snake that had woken early from hibernation. To finish off his awful day he was arrested for speeding while driving to hospital for treatment. (Oh well, some things never change.)

These human-interest stories, which appeared throughout the popular press, called the weather 'unusual', 'abnormal' or 'unseasonal'. But it was none of these things. The winter temperatures are fully in line with the scientific predictions. This is the new 'normal' weather.

And this was just the winter. Look what came later in 2007. April was the hottest ever recorded in Britain. Then the period May to July was the wettest since records began culminating in disastrous flooding across central and southern England. At the same time Greece and southern Europe had some of the hottest weather ever recorded and in Bulgaria 500 people died in one week in July from heatstroke.

And these are signs that we no longer have any option about being on this wretched ride. Our only option for the moment is how we choose to deal with it – do we ignore it and hope it will go away? Or do we decide to be positive and engage with it? And remember – we're still on the lift hill. The real ride hasn't even started yet.

Chapter 4

Over the top
The highlights of the ride

Our little car has been cranking up that lift hill, getting higher and higher, and as we reach the top for the first time we can see the climate ride laid out in front of us. Many parts are indistinct or hiding around a bend, but what we *can* see is that the track is going all over the place – up and down, left and right and loop the loop.

As I said earlier, the term 'global warming' is misleading. In reality the climate rollercoaster will throw its little cars all over the place. Although there is an overall direction – hotter and probably drier – we can expect all kinds of local weather. In some years there may be extreme cold as well as extreme heat. Snow may disappear in most places, but may fall harder in others. There may be floods one year and droughts the next.

And, as demonstrated throughout this book, changes in the weather will be mediated by the social and political response, which will either moderate or exaggerate their actual impacts.

The smart people in the car have twigged what is going on and what will be coming next. They realize that they are fully committed to the ride and are locked in tightly. But other people are still refusing to accept what is happening. They are ignoring the view and are chatting among themselves. Their straps are hanging loose.

So here we are at the very top. This is that scary bit of the ride, before we find out what all of that stored energy can do. There's no going back, no chance to change our minds or ask for our money back.

And – whooooooosh – over we go.

What is going to happen in the United Kingdom?

First of all: heat. The UK Climate Impacts Programme (UKCIP) is predicting a steady year-on-year increase in temperatures so that, by the 2050s, southern England will be 2.5°C (4.5°F) warmer. Extreme temperatures, such as occurred during the heatwave of 2003, which killed 2,000 people in the UK, will become a regular feature of our summers, which will be nearly one-third drier with regular droughts. The Association of British Insurers (ABI) is predicting that 4 million houses could be at risk from future subsidence owing to the increased drying of clay subsoils and that weather-damage claims will treble by 2050.

Snow and frost will have largely disappeared from southern England and will survive simply as a memory on Christmas cards. Within 15 years Mount Snowdon will become Mount 'Snowgone' as it loses all of its snow cover.

We may still dream of a white Christmas, but what we will get is mud. Winters will be up to 15 per cent wetter, and that extra rain will come down in far more violent downpours. The government estimates that by 2050, half a million people will be at risk of flooding in old cities where Victorian sewer systems, unable to cope with the extra load, will spill water and sewage into homes. Insurers are already noting a significant year-on-year increase of car accidents from extreme rainfall.

There will be a steady increase in sea level and storm surges. The existing Thames Barrier will be unable to cope after 2030, and the Thames Valley will be at risk of regular flooding. The east coast, especially Lincolnshire, will face regular flooding, and large areas of East Anglia and the Fens may be lost to the sea.

Wildlife will change dramatically. Those animals whose lifecycles are dependent on regular seasons will be severely affected. To cite just one example, blue tit populations are falling because their nesting season is no longer synchronized with the appearance of the caterpillar larvae they need to feed their young. Species that cannot move north fast enough will die out. Scottish plant and bird species face a particularly bleak future.

At the same time southern European species will be on the move and will start appearing in the UK. The first ever UK population of yellow-tailed scorpions has just been found in Kent. In 2004 there were the first ever sightings of great white sharks and the deadly Portuguese man-of-war jellyfish off the coasts of Devon and Cornwall.

In our gardens water-thirsty plants like roses may not be able to survive the drier summers with their inevitable hose-pipe bans. English Nature is now advising gardeners to plant Mediterranean shrubs.

What is going to happen to people in the rest of the world?

Far more severe things will be happening elsewhere in the world. In February 2007 the Intergovernmental Panel on

Climate Change (IPCC) – the body that consolidates and summarizes the scientific research – presented its 1,200-page Fourth Assessment Report. Every table, graph and statement has been picked over by 2,500 scientists who have drawn their conclusions with great caution. Maybe too much caution. Even the former chair of the IPCC scientific assessment panel, Sir John Houghton, said that it has 'deliberately underestimated the problem'.

So we can think of the report as an underestimate of the ride ahead for the rest of the world. Even so, it makes pretty dreadful reading. The IPCC predicts that the frequency of devastating storms will increase dramatically; snow will disappear from all but the highest mountains; deserts will spread; oceans will become acidic, leading to the destruction of coral reefs and atolls; and deadly heatwaves will become more prevalent.

Let's take just one of these predicted impacts, rising sea levels. The IPCC says sea levels are rising at the rate of almost 2 mm (⅛ in) a year and will probably rise by 50 cm (20 in) by the end of the century. Many experts believe that the IPCC may be severely underestimating the scale and speed of sea level rise. A recent paper by the Potsdam Institute for Climate Impact Research (PIK) says that sea levels could rise by well over a metre (3 feet) by 2100. A recent World Bank study found that a metre rise in sea levels would force about 60 million people in developing countries to abandon their homes, half of them in Bangladesh. Much of the Nile delta would be swamped as would large parts of Vietnam, including the Mekong delta. Closer to home, sea level rises could be twice as fast for East Anglia, which is sinking at 1.5 mm (¹⁄₁₆ in) per year. The UKCIP models suggest that by 2050 the annual flood-damage bill could run as high as £900 million for East

Anglia alone. And, whatever we do, sea levels will not stop rising for several thousand years.

But it doesn't end there. It now seems extremely unlikely that we can avoid the temperature increases required to melt the entire Greenland ice sheet. This contains so much water – it is 3 kilometres (1.9 miles) thick after all – that it will raise global sea levels by 7 metres (23 feet). The historical record supports this. Global temperatures 125,000 years ago were 3 degrees higher than now and sea levels were indeed 6 metres (19½ feet) higher.

How long the Greenland ice sheet will take to melt is a hotly debated topic. Many scientists, including James Hansen the lead climate change scientist for the National Aeronautics and Space Administration (NASA), are arguing that ice sheets could collapse rapidly over a period of a few hundred years and point out that this is what happened 14,000 years ago, at the end of the last ice age. Whatever the actual conclusions, it is worth noting that the Greenland glaciers are melting far, far faster than was previously predicted and overall sea level rise is already at the upper end of the IPCC predictions. And this is to say nothing of the Western Antarctic ice sheet, which is already breaking up and could potentially add an additional 5 metres (16 feet) to sea levels.

Now a 7 metre (23 foot) rise in sea level would drown most of central London. We may decide to spend hundreds of billions of pounds to protect it, but I can't imagine that anyone could defend all of the Florida coast. And, let's face it, there will be no defenses at all for the poorest countries.

They will have other problems, too. The World Health Organization (WHO) estimates that increases in infectious diseases directly attributable to climate change are already responsible for 150,000 additional deaths per year. It says that this number could double by 2030. Rice yields in some parts of Asia have already fallen by 10 per cent because of increased temperatures, and the yields of staple food crops in sub-Saharan Africa could fall by more than a third. In July 2006 the UK Department for International Development (DfID) announced that the impacts of climate change in Africa will cancel all the benefits of Western aid and debt relief. Major development organizations, including Oxfam and Christian Aid, now regard climate change as the greatest single threat to the world's poorest and most marginalized peoples.

What will happen to wildlife?

Let's look at the impact on the natural world. A string of scientific reports have predicted mass extinctions. A major study in 2004 estimated that, by mid-century, a quarter of all animal and plant species would be committed to extinction. Scientists are using that word 'committed' again, and it means that much of whatever is still around in 50 years is on death row with no chance of an appeal. Coral reefs will not be able to adapt fast enough to increasing sea temperatures and will largely die out, no matter what our response to climate change. Scientists in Australia are warning that the Great Barrier Reef will be 'functionally extinct' by 2030 – this means that it may still be holding on but it has little chance of survival.

Even more worrying are the uncertainties concerning the Amazon rainforest. It contains a quarter of the world's animal and plant species and plays a key role in regulating world climate and carbon dioxide flows. Computer models developed by the UK's Hadley Centre for Climate Prediction and Research indicate that the centre of Brazil will become increasingly dry, leading from 2040 onwards to the rapid conversion of the rainforest to open, dry forest. 'Rapid conversion' is a polite way of saying that it will burn down, and as it does so it will release billions of tonnes more carbon dioxide into the air.

And this leads us to the greatest long-term concern: that the increase in global temperatures could trigger the release of natural stores of carbon dioxide and methane in forests and soils, which would make matters even worse.

Heard enough?

This seems like a good place to stop. There is a great temptation to go into even greater detail, and there are many excellent studies – listed at the back of this book – that do so (see pages 316–9). However, I fear that I may already be provoking that Medusa effect I warned about. On its own, any one of the predictions sounds possible but daunting. When presented together the problem starts to sound too huge and dreadful, and we start to doubt its truth.

Well, I'm sorry to say, it is all true. Each of the above examples is drawn from very detailed research and analysis. Things might, just might, be better than this. On rare occasions scientists have downgraded their predictions. But the overwhelming tendency over the past ten years has been for new research not only to reinforce but to *increase* the IPCC predictions.

So my advice to you is this – accept that you are in for a rocky ride. The challenge for you is to find an attitude that will enable you to remain positive, focused and in the moment.

Chapter 5

Screaming and waving

How to find the right attitude for the climate rollercoaster

Rollercoasters are designed to scare us. The process by which we turn this terrifying experience into something pleasurable is entirely a matter of having the right attitude and sharing the experience with others.

When we go on a rollercoaster we are prepared mentally for what is coming. We have been on rides before and can anticipate what the experience will be like. Before getting on we look the ride over and see what it does.

Can you imagine how terrifying a rollercoaster would be if you had no idea what it was or what the outcome might be? All of your instincts would tell you that the rollercoaster was extremely dangerous and probably fatal. What would you do? Would you panic? If there were no strong strap to secure you, would you jump off and take your chances of surviving the landing?

Embrace your fear

A rollercoaster would be a dismal and disturbing experience if we had to do it on our own in silence. So we scream our lungs out, as does everyone else around us. Rollercoasters provide something very unusual in our society – they encourage us openly to share our fear of a frightening experience with strangers. This is especially unusual for us men, who spend our entire lives trying to hide our emotions. Read through coaster sites and time and again reviews mention the thrill of openly expressing fear.

Now that you are on the climate rollercoaster, the greatest ride of all, how you deal with it will also depend entirely on your attitude. You may prefer to ignore what is happening. As we discuss later, it is surprisingly easy to push all of the evidence to one side and pretend that nothing is happening. But I can promise you this – you cannot escape reality. You are on this ride and you *will* be thrown about just like everyone else. And if you are not ready for it, your whole life could be turned upside down, too: had you recognized and shared your fears with other people you could be prepared mentally for what was coming; because you did not, you may find yourself scared and panicking.

Surely it is always better to accept what it is coming and be as well informed and prepared as you can be. With forewarning you will have a healthy and positive attitude. You will be able to adapt and position yourself to make the most of it. And as we discover later in the book, you may even thrive.

As part of that acceptance you will be able to talk openly with others about your concerns and fears and enjoy their companionship and support. A wonderful feeling of comradeship and connection comes when people join together against great odds. Wouldn't you rather have that?

Chapter 6

You *will* be OK

Our chances of getting off safely

Hang on, you say, there is another condition that is crucial for our enjoyment of a rollercoaster ride. No matter how dangerous it *looks*, we trust that the device is basically safe, that the management would prefer to keep its customers alive and that we will be delivered safely and in one piece at the end.

It is hard to feel the same confidence about the climate rollercoaster. We will be the first people on it. It has never been tested and there is no guarantee of our safety. So it is important that you take my word for it: for this first ride at any rate:

You will be OK. You may be shaken but you will survive the worst that climate change throws at you

Yes there are some extreme and dangerous things coming on this ride. There may be major impacts on your life. The economy may very well suffer. And it is inevitable that extreme weather will claim some victims. But our capacity to deal with climate change will also improve. Humans will adjust, adapt and defend themselves just as they always have done.

You must ignore the dramatic fantasies that appear in films and newspapers. Humans will not be wiped out. The Earth is never going to turn into Venus. You will be OK

But I should add two very important conditions. First, I can promise your safety because you live in a rich, industrialized country with a moderate climate. You are well protected. People living in the poorest countries – who are already on the edge of survival – are not: millions of them could die from disease, famine and disasters. Second, if we do not reduce our emissions within this generation all bets are off.

Chapter 7

And off we go again
Why the rollercoaster never stops

It's been a long and wild ride, lasting for decades, maybe the rest of your life. Finally your little rickety car comes to a stop. You are shaken and wobbling from the experience, but, as I promised, you are still in one piece.

You get out . . . and your grandchildren get in. This ride is not going to end for a long time yet. Just as we are already committed to the ride, so too will be future generations. At least your grandchildren will be better warned and better prepared than you were. Their car gets smaller and smaller as it cranks up the incline that starts the ride. The big question is this: how high is this rollercoaster now?

It all depends on what we do. Like the rollercoaster, the world's climate systems are powered by the energy put in at the front end. If we are smart we will stabilize concentrations of the greenhouse gases in the atmosphere. It will certainly be a different world – with hotter temperatures and higher sea levels – but the global climate will find a new equilibrium, and after a difficult period of adaptation we will find ways to live in a changed world.

Because there is a time-lag built into the world's climate systems we will have to live with the effects of the greenhouse gases that have already been put into the air by our parents and grandparents. But if we don't reduce our emissions, the rollercoaster will get higher and higher. We are in a strange situation: we have little say over our present but a huge say over the future.

With concerted action we can stabilize the situation – we may even find a better way to live. But if we refuse to change, we will create an awful future. Imagine how it would feel to wave goodbye to your grandchildren on a ride that is so high and so shaky that you can no longer see the top and there is no longer any guarantee that the little cars will stay on the tracks? This is why we all need to act now to reduce emissions.

Overcoming denial and truly believing in climate change

Chapter 1
The lost years
Why it took me so long to believe in climate change

In October 2005 I was standing on my back porch having a cigarette when I realized that climate change was really happening. Like many smokers I have an off-and-on relationship with cigarettes. I like to claim that a plus side to smoking is that I get more fresh air, although admittedly I am doing everything I can to stop it getting inside my body.

It was a clear night, and as I stood looking at the stars I felt the warm evening breeze blowing across me. I bathed in its moist, rich fertile smell, recalling fond memories of holidays in Italy. The only thing missing was a background buzz of crickets.

And then I felt a violent shudder running all through my body – as if I had been wired to the mains. It was an overwhelming sense of danger that triggered all of my animal defence mechanisms – my hairs stood on end, my skin started sweating, my heart was pounding. My body had heard the warning carried by that gentle breeze. This wasn't some balmy garden on the Adriatic – it was a dingy backyard on an Oxford housing estate. And it was late October – we should already have had the first frost. It later turned out that this had been the hottest October weather on record.

In that instant, and for the first time, I *truly* believed in climate change. You could say that, after a long slumber, I had woken up and found myself on the rollercoaster.

Now when I tell this story, most people look at me as if I am nuts. 'What has this got to do with climate change,' they think, 'and what was he *really* smoking.' One time I told my story at a public meeting on climate change and the next speaker got quite angry. 'I think all this talk about belief is just wasting our time,' he said, 'what we need is action.'

But when I tell my story to people with a religious faith they understand immediately what I mean and why I am telling it. They understand that you can spend years going through the motions and say all the right things without truly believing something in your heart. And they recognize that true belief can come at strange times and in an instant of transcendental awareness. I wouldn't call my porch revelation a religious experience as such, but I must say that it shared many of the same qualities.

Not only did this experience leave me deeply shaken but it raised a disturbing question: if, in that instant, I had suddenly and truly believed in climate change, did this mean that I had been working on something for five years that I didn't actually believe in?

And the answer has to be 'yes'. Now this does not mean that my work was ineffective because of that. In some ways it might have been more effective. The few people who I can say without question truly believe in climate change have an alarming tendency to grab people by the lapels and scream at them – and this is not a very effective way to communicate their concerns. But it was also clear that belief in climate change is not a switch – it exists in degrees, and it takes years to acquire.

My own, slow journey

It had taken me 13 years to get this far, and it would take me another five before I had the doorstep epiphany that finally hammered it home. I had first heard about climate change in 1987, at a small public meeting given by Quaker Peace and Justice. The lady who presented it was in her 50s, very calm and reasonable and measured, and very clear about the vast new threats that were unfolding. I was staggered. I bombarded her with questions and demanded to know why people were doing so little about it. And then I did nothing.

For years I kept hearing about it. And still I did nothing. I was having a fun life, and there wasn't much room for new issues. But in retrospect I know that I was also caught up in the same collective mass denial as everyone else. Outside the fringes of the green movement, very few people were talking about climate change. It rarely made the papers and never appeared in conversations. Had I been asked what I thought of it, I would have said that it was very serious but I wasn't letting that opinion affect any aspect of my behaviour. By the late 1990s I was working in New York and regularly zipped back home to catch up with family and friends. I once flew back just for a date – a hot date, mind you.

In 2000, after some serious thought, the scale and importance of the issue finally sunk in, and I made a life-changing decision to change my career and work on nothing else. Although I was ahead of the curve, this was hardly any great insight on my part. It had taken me 13 years to get this far and I still had a long way to go before I really believed in it.

What all of this tells me is that knowing about climate change is not the same as believing in it. Yet every book, report, leaflet, scientific conference and government statement on climate change assumes that as soon as we receive the information we act on it.

When they find that people aren't doing anything, they put it down to a failure in *communication* and respond with more data, louder messages, zappier slogans and smarter presentations. They assume that, if only people knew *how* serious it was they would listen. So they commission new reports and speak in stronger and more apocalyptic tones.

At this point all of the denial mechanisms start kicking in. Some people immediately reject bad news. Some refuse to believe it. And most people accept it and file it away as 'one of those problems that someone should do something about'.

In this section I ask you to think in a very different way about climate change

I ask you to think long and hard about any factors that might be making it hard for you fully to accept climate change. You may need to work hard to keep your belief and your determination going in the face of the denial of your friends, family and society as a whole. But it is crucial that you do. If you are going to engage effectively with climate change, you must seek to build a well-grounded belief. Only then can you consider what you may wish to do about it.

Chapter 2

The blind leading the blind

Why most of the people warning us about climate change still don't believe in it

I am convinced that most of the people warning us about climate change do not fully believe in what they are saying. This does not mean that what they are saying is untrue or unreliable, just that they themselves find it hard to accept.

Tony Blair, for example, found it impossible to make any connection between an issue he described as 'so irreversible in its destructive power, that it alters radically human existence' and the ways that he personally contributes to it. In 2006 he had three foreign holidays – in Italy, Barbados and Florida.

Well, we might say, 'Politician doesn't do what he tells others to do' isn't a headline that will sell many newspapers. But we would expect climate scientists and environmentalists to be more connected to the issues they work on.

Some examples of conflicting behaviour

Two years ago I spoke at a packed public meeting alongside a senior scientist from the British Antarctic Survey. He gave a strong and clear outline of the threats of climate change and the changes that we would all need to make. Later, in the pub, he admitted that he flies several times a year on skiing holidays, most recently to the Chilean Andes. He knew only too well how destructive those flights were, but he said he found his job very stressful and he needed the break. I was staggered. His break from the cold and ice is flying around the world to find more cold and ice? How much snow does this man need?

Another pub moment. Three years earlier I was sitting at a table in the basement bar of Greenpeace International's headquarters with its climate change campaign team. (Now whatever you think of Greenpeace, you have to admit that an in-house bar is pretty damned smart). They were talking about which airlines give them the best air-miles scheme. The head of the Greenpeace US climate change campaign had no doubt. She flew so often with United that she had earned their 'gold key pass', which gave her an automatic upgrade to business class. The co-ordinator of an international campaign against oil companies had just come back from holiday – scuba diving in the Pacific.

I wouldn't call any of these people hypocrites. I don't doubt their commitment to this issue or the value of their work. However, at a personal level they are clearly finding it hard fully to match up what they know with what they do. They may work on climate change for a living, but they are just like the rest of us. In opinion polls 85 per cent of us say that climate change is a serious or a very serious issue. And yet we buy ever larger cars and houses, fly ever further and use ever more energy.

Since the 1970s British household energy demand has risen by 1½ to 2 per cent every year. During that period we have had two major oil shocks, the Rio environment conference, the Kyoto Protocol, the twenty hottest years on record and the strongest hurricanes, heat waves and downpours in recorded history. And yet none of these events has triggered the slightest wobble in that demand for domestic energy. Each of these events was a sign saying 'slow down – cliff coming', and we accelerated through each one of them. We see them but we don't believe them.

Over the next ten chapters I explore the reasons why we find it so hard to believe in climate change. I argue that, fundamentally, the problem is configured in such a way that bypasses our inbuilt danger-detection mechanisms. So we can 'know' that it is dangerous but we find it very hard to 'feel' that it is.

Because we do not *feel* the danger we are not under any pressure to take personal action. Although we *know* that we need to do something, we create all kinds of elaborate personal excuses to avoid the challenge to change.

These mechanisms are complex and deep, and we are often unaware that they even operate. But knowing about them and recognizing how they work are the first real steps to coming to terms with climate change and taking action.

In this section I do not ask you to do anything at all – I do not ask you to change. All I ask is that you consider the arguments and reflect upon them. Are these your obstacles, and if they are, how can you best overcome them? I can't provide answers for everyone, but at least I hope that, in raising these issues, I can encourage you to be more self-aware and, through this, more effective.

Chapter 3

Be unnatural

Why we need to bypass our natural defences

All of us carry within us a 'risk thermostat' that warns us of threats and helps us to choose an appropriate response. Every day, especially in the stressful urban environment, we are negotiating with our risk thermostat. For example:

I notice a car is coming down the road straight towards me.
   Is he going to run me down?
He looks like he really *is* going to try to run me down. This is dangerous.
   Do I stand my ground or do I back down?
I think I'll move to one side and scream at him. Oh no he has stopped and climbed out of the car and is coming back up the road towards me. He looks unpleasant.
   Is he a nut?
He's bright purple and his fists are clenched. He is a nut. And he's still dangerous.
   Do I stay and fight it out?
Think I'll scarper.

(And that was just my cycle ride to work this morning.)

These warnings and responses were determined by psychological conditioning that has been formed, tried and tested by the previous problems we've encountered over millennia of psychological evolution. As in this case, the thermostat is triggered fastest by threats that are visible, immediate, comprehensible, involve personal physical damage and have a clear cause. As competitive social animals, we are very experienced in dealing with problems caused by an identifiable human enemy and can rapidly access a wide range of possible responses.

So far so good, but I am sure you are already sensing where I am going with this. Climate change has *none* of the qualities I list above – qualities that trigger the risk thermostat. It is invisible. It develops slowly and steadily over a long period. It might threaten direct physical damage, but it is not at all clear who will be hurt or what will happen to them. It is unlike any situation that we have encountered before and requires intellectual abstraction and imagination to comprehend.

But the biggest problem with climate change is that it has no single identifiable enemy against whom we can mobilize. Everyone in the industrialized world is the enemy causing the problem, including our family and best friends. We are the enemy.

Look at it another way

Imagine how different our response to climate change would be if it did have a single identifiable cause. Suppose that the CIA found that North Korea was releasing chemicals into the air designed to permanently alter the world's climate. Climate scientists confirmed that these chemicals had already led to a 50 per cent increase in the formation of hurricanes in the Gulf of Mexico. And then, while these revelations were being made public, imagine that Hurricane Katrina hit New Orleans.

We know only too well what would happen. I suspect that the only protest marches would be those demanding faster action. Hurricane Katrina would be regarded as an act of war, and the US would respond accordingly with the full support of the international community. There would be no objections to the cost of the response, whether economic or human.

So, if climate change were caused by North Korea, it would be perfectly configured to trigger our risk thermostats. It would have an enemy, a motive, a violent act and a means of effective response. It would play perfectly to all of our *natural* responses.

It's not easy being beige

Now normally we are urged to **be natural**. That's the message drummed into our heads by all those books on health, environment and lifestyle. I have many friends who wholeheartedly subscribe to this creed, turning the insides of their bedsits into rustic huts of open-weave natural fibres, curing themselves with twig extracts that they drink out of wobbly hand-thrown pots and dressing entirely in unbleached 'natural' fabrics. They are very sympathetic to the environment, but I wouldn't really call them green – actually they are more beige than anything else. Endless shades of sepia and light sienna with the odd highlight of terracotta.

It's all pretty harmless. Many of the 'beige' ideas are good models for low-carbon living, and it usually does make sense for us to be more 'natural'

But though we might need to live more naturally, our thinking about climate change is going to have to be as unnatural as a polystyrene cup. We are going to have to ignore our trusted risk thermostat and recognize that it is malfunctioning. We are going to have to construct new ways of thinking and dealing with this problem that play to our desire to co-operate rather than our desire to compete.

Chapter 4

Smokescreens

Want to understand climate-change denial? Ask a smoker

The smokers are all lined up along the bar, and the little packs in front of them carry the chilling phrase 'smoking kills' written down the side. They might as well be perched on their stools sipping toilet cleaner.

As I have said, I am an on-and-off smoker. When I start smoking again my wife Annie feigns a sympathetic tone. 'Poor George,' she says, 'it really is a struggle for you, isn't it?' She can afford to be condescending because I refused to marry her unless she stopped smoking. She succeeded and I failed. So, like all prevaricators, I have been busy renegotiating the agreement: 'Technically,' I point out to her, 'I am not actually a smoker. I am a non-smoker who sometimes has a cigarette – and that is something very different.' Clearly I am well qualified to understand the denial strategies of smokers.

What's my excuse?
We smokers all know it is a problem but find complex arguments for not dealing with it. All of these strategies

apply to the ways that we avoid dealing with climate change:

It's a long way off yet

Smokers conveniently locate all the serious health impacts of smoking at some point in the distant future. All smokers assume that they will stop before they reach that point but, strangely, the time to stop never comes. Even the knowledge of the pain of cancer cannot persuade them to abandon the 'pleasure' of feeding their addiction. Psychologists note that this tendency to 'discount' future losses is very strong, especially in our culture. After all, the entire hire-purchase and credit-card industries are based on the principle of buy-now-pay-later.

It won't happen to me

Smokers like to believe that it is always other people who die of cancer. Although the odds are terrifying, there is no *certainty* that a smoker will contract lung cancer or have a heart attack. The warning on the packet says 'smoking kills' but it doesn't say 'smoking will kill *you*', and smokers exploit these uncertainties. Like all of us, they have a natural tendency to read odds in a way that favours a pleasant outcome. For example, we buy lottery tickets even though the odds of winning the jackpot are 1 in 14 million. The chances of being hit and killed by a meteorite over the course of your lifetime are 30 times higher, but we don't give it a second thought.

When assessing danger, we prioritize large-scale and dramatic events that we can readily imagine. In the US 440,000 smokers die each year in hospital wards and hospices. If they had all died in a single dramatic event the risks would be far more apparent. After all, this is 160 times more people than died in the attack on the World Trade Center.

I don't want to lose my one pleasure

Smokers define their nicotine addiction as a 'pleasure', even though they stopped enjoying it years ago. They then fixate on the idea that stopping smoking will be about *giving up* this pleasure rather than *gaining* health or extra life. Psychologically, we feel losses far more painfully than gains, which is why addicts only truly change behaviour when they perceive that the pain of continuing their addiction is greater than the pain of stopping.

I'm a smoker

People create their self-image around the act of smoking. They are assisted by the embedded memory of smoking role models, and the underlying perceptions that smoking is cool or sexy or fun-loving or sociable. These perceptions become deeply engrained and are impervious to any observation that smokers can also be ugly, miserable or loners.

In my case, I started smoking because it was what the bad kids at school did. By seeing myself as a 'smoker' I was also making a strong statement that I was not like the 'cleanies' or the 'sporties' or the parents or the teachers. As we shall see, we very often define ourselves as what we are not.

Can I have one of yours?

Sometimes I find myself craving a cigarette but will not admit to myself that I am hooked again. So I resort to an ingenious strategy known to all on-and-off smokers: I smoke other people's cigarettes. During this delusional phase, I scrounge remorselessly off friends, start up conversations with people I don't like in the hope of being offered a cigarette or even go up to total strangers in pubs and offer to buy one. I have no shame nor feel the slightest hint of embarrassment. After all, they are helping me to meet my craving without becoming a smoker again – and that's a good thing. Right?

What's your excuse?

All of the strategies that smokers use to avoid facing the risks of their addiction have direct parallels in our response to climate change.

First of all, we tend to define climate change as a problem for other people in the future. In polls more people say that climate change is a threat for future generations or other countries than a threat to themselves now. The victims we imagine (and are encouraged to imagine) are in poor countries or are polar bears, not our own elderly dying of heatstroke.

Because the impacts of climate change are dispersed and hard to imagine we tend greatly to underestimate their scale in comparison to higher profile threats, such as terrorism. It is interesting that American public concern about climate change leapt following the devastation of Hurricane Katrina because, for the first time, people could assess its risk in terms of a dramatic and knowable event.

When told that we will need to change the way we live, we often see it as a matter of giving something up rather than gaining something better. And, like smokers, many of the things that we fear losing, especially cars and flights, are deeply engrained in our minds as 'pleasures', even if we find them unsatisfying or unpleasant.

Like smokers, we define ourselves around our high-carbon habits. Our lifestyles are such a powerful statement of who we are that many people feel actively threatened by suggestions that they could live differently. They see it as a criticism of who they are and a pressure to become someone they are not. Telling a shopping addict that she can live with less is about as effective as telling the rebels puffing away around the back of the bike sheds that they should be more like the school prefects. It is not very effective communication.

And finally, when we recognize the overall problem but refuse to admit to our addiction, we find all kinds of sneaky ways to transfer responsibility to someone else, just like the cigarette scroungers. If we feel guilty about our holiday flight but want to make it anyway, we can pay money to carbon offset companies to install low-energy lightbulbs in some shantytown. They reduce emissions and we keep flying.

At an international level, there is now a vast, new, carbon-trading market on which major polluters can buy and sell 'carbon credits'. British Airways argues that there is no need to reduce the amount we fly because it can buy up 'carbon credits' from companies that have reduced their emissions. It's a strategy that will require a lot more charm than BA can muster.

But there is a positive side to this comparison. It should be much easier to cut out carbon than cut out cigarettes. Nicotine is one of the most addictive chemicals we know and constantly nags for replenishment.

Dealing with climate change is hardly in the same league. You don't wake up in the middle of the night with a desperate desire to turn on the heating and every light in the house – not unless you are an insomniac, anyway.

The lifestyle decisions that lead us to our high emissions are *habits* not addictions. They can be deeply engrained in our behaviour and self-image but, once they are challenged, they lose their hold over us.

Chapter 5

Stifling your inner sceptic

How you can resist the climate change deniers

Had I written the previous chapter forty years ago I would have added one more strategy that smokers use to avoid dealing with their addiction.

The dangers are only a theory

Smokers know that there is growing scientific evidence that smoking causes life-threatening diseases, but they prefer to believe that it is still a matter for debate and that the science is unsettled. They are strongly encouraged to believe this by the tobacco industry, which pours millions of dollars into quasi-scientific front groups and research designed to undermine the medical consensus.

In 1954, when the first strong evidence emerged of a connection between smoking and lung cancer, the US tobacco companies placed a full-page advertisement in 448 newspapers stating that 'there is no proof that cigarette smoking is one of the causes of lung cancer'. To back up this claim, they formed the seemingly independent Tobacco Industry Research Committee (TIRC), which hired scientists and doctors to argue against the scientific evidence on the health impacts of smoking. Their strategy was not to win the argument but to create the impression that the science had not been settled. As a memo from the tobacco company Brown and Williamson noted, 'Doubt is our product since it is the best means of competing with the "body of fact" that exists in the mind of the general public.'

Forty years later, when US oil and coal companies felt threatened by the growing scientific consensus on climate change, they reproduced the same tried-and-tested tactics. Between 1998 and 2005 Exxon Mobil alone poured $16 million into think-tanks and bogus research groups that argued that climate change was not serious, was not proven or was not caused by human activity.

From the late 1990s onwards a small handful of professional pundits began to appear with alarming regularity in the British media, usually in staged debates against real scientists. Not all of them are funded directly by oil and coal companies. Some are motivated by a deep loathing for environmentalism. Some are failed academics enjoying the spotlight for the first time. And some are people whose careers are in the doldrums and who want to be back in that spotlight.

However, regardless of their personal motivations or feigned independence, they are linked together as one network. They write books together, sit on the boards of each other's front organizations, give each other grants, appear on the same conference podia or on the same websites, borrow each other's arguments and quote each other's 'research'. They like to call themselves 'sceptics', suggesting the independent and critical analysis of free thinkers and outsiders. A better description, albeit less pithy, would be 'opportunistic, self-promoting climate change deniers'. I have met or debated against most of them, and, as you can tell, they are not my favourite people.

However, they are often very persuasive because they are professional communicators, and they can be enthusiastic and charming. They can pick whatever arguments they think best suit their case, whether they are true or not. In debates they are usually put up against real scientists who, let's face it, are rarely great speakers. It is like a court case where a top barrister leads the prosecution and a librarian leads the defence. Of course they win the arguments.

Now, be honest. Have you ever heard and been swayed by any of the following arguments?

'The scientists are still undecided'

No, they are not. Every scientific institution in the world accepts that climate change is caused by human activity and says so regularly. There are 2,500 scientists who report to the Intergovernmental Panel on Climate Change, and their conclusions are rigorously challenged. Claims that thousands of scientists disagree are falsified: the number of qualified practising climate scientists who disagree with the consensus is tiny and shrinking. They are as marginal as 'scientists' who claim that black people are less intelligent or that evolution does not exist. The news media love the debate format, but it gives a totally false sense of the balance of opinion.

'There are still uncertainties'

Yes, there are plenty of uncertainties. The world's climate system is very complex, and the predicted impacts sit in a very wide range. But there is not one model that says that there will be no impacts. Even the lowest level of the predictions is serious, and all the indications are that we are going to experience the higher end.

'This graph, chart, table, piece of 'research', shows that carbon dioxide is not causing climate change'

There are repeated claims that the increase in world temperatures is being caused by something else: sun spots or cosmic rays or a change in the earth's tilt or the CIA or who knows what. The problem is this: if something else is causing climate change, what is all of that carbon dioxide doing?

No one denies that carbon dioxide is a powerful greenhouse gas that retains heat in the atmosphere. Any rival theory about climate change has to explain why 40 per cent more carbon dioxide is making no difference to world temperatures. And not one of them can do this.

'The solutions to climate change will cost more than the impacts'

This argument, championed by the Danish academic Bjorn Lomborg in his book *The Sceptical Environmentalist* and innumerable interviews, sounds very reasonable. He accepts that climate change is serious but argues that the costs of reducing emissions will be far higher than the costs of adapting to the impacts. Lomborg's claims have been seriously attacked by his colleagues and by other academics – remember that he is a statistician not an economist.

In 2006 the British government commissioned Professor Nicholas Stern, the former head economist to the World Bank, to evaluate the relative economic costs of reducing emissions or suffering the impacts of climate change. Stern took 575 pages of data and analysis (as opposed to Lomborg's 20) to conclude that if we do not reduce our emissions, we risk 'major disruption to economic and social activity, on a scale similar to those associated with the great wars and the economic depression of the first half of the 20th century'. And even this sobering assessment does not even begin to account for the suffering of subsistence farmers in the world's poorest countries whose livelihoods barely register in economic models.

The reason why self-publicists such as Lomborg get such a positive hearing is that we feel short-term losses more painfully that long-term gains. He is telling us that if we change our behaviour we stand to gain little and lose a lot. There's one group of people who use this argument all the time to avoid changing their behaviour. Addicts.

Time to face your inner sceptic

I don't want to go into any more detail about specific deniers or their arguments. What is much more my concern is the effect that they have had on you. If you have accepted any of the arguments of the climate change denial industry – and there are many more – they have successfully created a sceptic mentality inside you that will reject, deflect or ignore the real and strong evidence of the problem. The dangerous sceptic is not the one who appears on TV but the one inside your own head. So this is not an argument with sceptics, it is an argument with your inner sceptic.

If you are a Traditionalist you may be especially vulnerable to sceptic arguments because they will offer the hope that the 'change' in climate change has been exaggerated. Sceptics often appear in the guise of middle-aged academics, which is deeply reassuring to

Traditionalists, and they are strongly promoted by the Traditionalist press, especially the *Daily Mail* and *Daily Telegraph*.

The first step to accepting climate change is to stifle your inner sceptic

Remember: of course there *will* be uncertainties. There *will* be exaggerations and false alarms. This is a rapidly changing field. But none of this undermines the fundamental truth of climate change.

When you encounter someone with arguments that disagree with the scientific consensus, don't let your judgement be swayed by the persuasiveness of the person putting the argument forward. Ask yourself: What is their motive? Do they have any legitimacy or any support from real experts? Why do I really want to believe what they say? And if they seem to be scientists from a legitimate university just look them up on the Internet and you will instantly find page after page of detailed information about their real activities.

Above all, remember the history of the tobacco industry. Forty years on and millions of premature deaths later, the misinformation campaign has failed. No smoker holds any hope that the science is unsettled or that smoking does not cause cancer. Misinformation campaigns that serve vested interests always lose in the end, but we will need to win this one a lot faster.

Chapter 6

Bad messengers

Why we find it hard to trust the people who warn us about climate change

There are four main providers of information on climate change: scientists, environmentalists, the media and politicians. All of them have their own agendas and, as any cynic could point out, their own particular reasons to be untrustworthy. I think it is fair to say that there is not a single person who would happily believe all four of them.

The scientists

Of the group, scientists are probably the most trusted. However, even if you can tell the difference between the real scientists and the professional climate change deniers – which is not easy – you still have to be able to interpret what they are saying. Scientists are cautious about drawing firm conclusions, and this is rightly a central principle of their profession. In a climate change debate on television you can easily spot the scientist in the pay of some oil company because he will be speaking with utter confidence and certainty. The real scientist will preface his conclusions with dithering caveats, such as 'although there are many uncertainties remaining, our data suggests a high probability that . . .'.

So scientists need translators to extract and promote the real and reliable messages from their work. This is where the problems start because the people who try to convert their research into a publicly digestible form are environmentalists and journalists. And they are two of the least trusted groups in society.

The environmentalists

The social subgroup of Anarcho Fogey Mincetarians doesn't respond well to labels, but I suppose that under duress I would admit to being an 'environmentalist'. So I write as an insider.

To give us our credit, we have doggedly pursued the climate issue for 20 years while everyone else has sat it out. For most of this time there has been virtually no engagement in the issue from trade unionists, the clergy, artists and musicians or anyone concerned with human rights, Third World development, refugees, social justice or armed conflict.

As a result, climate change is universally identified as an 'environmental' issue. It is reported by an environment correspondent, shelved in the environmental section of the bookshop and described by the environment minister as 'the biggest environmental problem we face'. Left to our own devices, we environmentalists have stamped our own identity on it. The images, language and issues of climate change are all drawn from the interests and campaign culture of environmentalism.

Steve Hounsham, who advises green groups on how to communicate climate change, argues that we have taken our lessons from the old TV series *Dad's Army*. There's Private Fraser saying over and over 'We're all doomed!' There's Sergeant Wilson putting on a superior air and criticizing what people do: 'Do you really think that's wise?' And then there's Corporal Jones running around in circles shouting, 'Don't panic! Don't panic!' And if this is what we are saying about ourselves, we can imagine what our enemies say.

The problem is that environmentalists are lobbyists and campaigners. We are selective about what we say and highly strategic in how we say it. The large environmental organizations are overwhelmingly dependent on personal donations, and their primary objective will always be to appeal to current or potential members.

Now, if you are in our constituency or sympathetic to a green view of the world, then you will be receptive to what we say. But you only have to go to any green event, even the most radical ones, to realize how limited that constituency is: it is still overwhelmingly white and middle class and usually middle aged. Although the green organizations have a combined membership of hundreds of thousands, the vast majority of people still do not identify with environmentalism. Of the personality types we met in Part 2, Winners are particularly averse to environmentalists, whom they tend to regard as earnest killjoys and bores.

But often people apply these derogatory labels to climate change as an excuse for not listening. By seeing climate change as an 'eco' issue people can define it as something that does not concern them or is relevant to their world view.

The journalists

These messengers are even less regarded. Newspapers have been crying 'wolf' for so long that nothing they say can be entirely trusted. During the past few years we have had screaming panic headlines telling us that we will all go insane from mad cow disease, cough to death from bird flu or face global economic collapse because computers couldn't change their dates.

The media coverage of climate change is frequently histrionic. Recent moderate and well-measured UK headlines have included 'It's worse than we thought', '10 years to save ourselves' and 'Countdown to global apocalypse'. What is worse, there is a crucial inconsistency in newspaper coverage, which guarantees that any serious article on the need for emissions reductions will be undermined by a breathless piece of puff on the next page discussing the wonders of a weekend break in Rio or the latest Mercedes luxury saloon.

My personal favourite is the issue of the *Independent* from 5 November 2005. Under the banner headline 'The melting mountains' a three-page special feature reported that 'climatologists predict the complete failure of the Alpine ski industry within 50 years'. The travel supplement in the same issue was an 11-page guide to the 50 best ski resorts. I suppose you could try one a year until you are skiing on gravel.

The politicians

What of our final messenger, the politicians? Does anyone trust politicians? Do their mothers trust them? 72 per cent of people say that they don't trust politicians at all. When you hear that Tony Blair says that climate change is the biggest threat we face, do you think, 'Gosh that must be serious' or do you think, 'Sure Tony, that and the Iraqi rockets that can hit us within 45 minutes'?

So, who do we trust? The answer is the same now as it has always been: the people we trust most are the people we know. As any advertiser can tell you, the most powerful advertisement for any car is that your next-door neighbour has one.

Avoiding the issue

This doesn't mean that we automatically trust what our friends, colleagues and neighbours say. After all, I will bet that your mates know about as much about the world's climate systems as they do about Schopenhauer's principle of sufficient reason. What the people we know *do* give us are cues about are the things that we should be paying attention to, the things that we should ignore and the conclusions that we should draw. This information-processing mechanism is so significant and powerful that sociologists created a special term for it: 'the constructed norms of attention'.

Several detailed studies into public attitudes to climate change have drawn the same disturbing conclusion: without ever talking about it, we have reached a collective agreement that climate change is outside our 'norms of attention'. Even though most people are well aware of the scientific warnings, it is still rarely considered appropriate to raise climate change in a conversation, even in a conversation about 'the funny weather we've been having'.

What a lovely spinach tart

Mayer Hillman, one of Britain's leading thinkers on climate

change, tells the story of sitting at a dinner party with globally concerned liberal people. Everyone was talking about their latest holiday trips, and Mayer could not resist bringing up the issue of climate change and the impacts of their flights. The room went very quiet until a guest decided to break the ice. 'My word,' she said, 'what a *lovely* spinach tart.' Oh yes, everyone agreed emphatically, it was a *very lovely* spinach tart. As Mayer says, the greatest denial strategy is silence – the deliberate collective decision not to talk about or engage with climate change.

Why do people who know about climate change, and tell opinion polls that they are seriously concerned, refuse to discuss it?

I suspect that this is a standard response when people feel that issues challenge their moral and social certainties. Societies undergoing mass human-rights abuses exhibit a remarkably similar selection of what is, or is not, acceptable to discuss.

Under Apartheid in South Africa there was a strong taboo in mainstream white society against discussing any racial or political concerns. People retreated into their private lives, cut themselves off from the news media and adopted an intense immersion in private diversions such as sport, holidays and families. In 1970s Brazil, during a time of aggressive state suppression and institutionalized torture, people even gave this process a name: innerism.

To believe in climate change you have to listen to the message, even if you don't trust the messenger

You need to recognize that this is an issue that transcends normal politics. Newspapers you would not normally read, politicians from a party you would not normally support and organizations that you might not normally listen to may well all be saying something very relevant and important.

You need to recognize that an issue can be of great importance without becoming a topic for accepted discussion with family friends, neighbours or workmates. Just because they are not openly registering it, does not mean that they are not interested or concerned.

And you have to be prepared to listen. You would go mad if you believed everything awful that you heard, so you have developed good filtering systems that tell you to stop listening. 'It's just a scare story,' you tell yourself. 'They're just saying that to sell newspapers.' 'She doesn't really believe that – she's just stirring things up.'

But when you hear something about climate change, you need to lower those defenses. Ask whether you can trust what they are saying, whether they speak with the backing of a reputable scientific publication or institution, and if they do, be prepared to really take on board what you hear.

Chapter 7

The pick-and-mix stand

How we collect ready-made excuses for not listening

We've already looked at some of the main reasons why we find it hard to deal with climate change.

• We have seen how, as a problem, it is perfectly configured to confound our natural risk thermostat. It is long drawn out, invisible, complex and with no clear enemy.

• We have seen how, like smokers, we can adopt a range of arguments to avoid dealing with a problem that seems to be a long way off and requires personal change.

• We have seen how we can reject a message because we don't like the messenger.

These were general observations that apply to all people. Now let's get more personal.

Time to face facts

You can think of these excuses presented as a 'pick-and-mix' sweet stand, like the sort they have in Woolworths. If you are thrilled by the thought of a hundred different kinds of pickled herring, you could think of it as a smorgasbord of Scandinavian delicacies. Or if, like me, your favourite deadly sin is gluttony, you could think of it as a mile-long Las Vegas eat-till-you-explode buffet.

The combination of arguments people actually choose from the pick-and-mix stand will depend on their personality type, tastes, politics, life experience and, above all, everything they've been told by parents, society and advertisers about who they are and who they should be.

Taken together, these values provide a personal 'frame' on the world that selects the information that is relevant to them, the products they buy and the actions they take. When they receive information on a new issue, it is this pre-existing framework that decides whether they should pay any attention at all and what they should do.

And in the case of climate change, they won't have to work very hard to find the arguments for not dealing with it, because they are all around them already. All they need to do is open up their paper bag and drop them in.

And I will bet that no matter how much you are concerned about climate change some of these excuses are used by you too. You are also human, and everyone, even professional scientists, finds it hard to believe in climate change and finds excuses for playing it down.

So now we've sat down on the wall outside Woolies and I'm looking inside your paper bag. Be honest, which of the following arguments would I find in there?

We're all stuffed

Yes, it's awful isn't it, but kind of thrilling, too. I guess we're really going to stuff things up. Oh well, the cockroaches can take over.

There's nothing I can do
I'm only one tiny part of all this. There's really nothing meaningful that I can do, especially when you look at how big it is and how small I am.

It's not illegal yet
I suppose the government will step in and ban it at some point, but, hey, let's do what we want while we can.

This isn't the real issue
Why are you banging on so much about climate change? The real issues are poverty, injustice, racism, terrorism. These are much more urgent issues, and I can't see us doing anything about climate change until we sort them out.

Bring on the boffins
They'll find a way to sort it out. They always do. They'll put big mirrors in space or build a big kind of vacuum cleaner thing that can suck it all back out of the air. Or something.

The wonders of capitalism
Calm down, madam! The market is already sorting it out. There are clear market signals that are producing a rapidly increasing inflow of investment into emissions reduction and technological innovation. And we can find ways to trade any of the problems away.

I've got enough problems
Yes, it sounds bad and I would like to do something, but I'm so busy and I've got a lot happening in my life and it really is as much as I can do to keep it together without having something else to worry ... DANIEL! Put that down NOW!

It's all looking up

Well, a few years ago I would have been much more worried, but now things have really changed, what with Al Gore's film and all those windmills everywhere, and I heard about an eco-city thing in Shanghai, and all the politicians are talking about it. Seems like it's all under way.

Don't take away my toys

I've worked hard for what I have and it's taken a long time to get to where I am now. I'm not giving it away or sharing it with anyone one, especially not *you*.

You have no right to tell me what to do

I'll bet you're no different. So how do you heat your house then Mr Eco Smartypants? With my taxes, I'll bet.

And it gets worse

There are four arguments in particular that are so common and so powerful that I have pulled them out for more attention in the next few chapters. I will bet that most people will have at least one of the following in their bag.

Costa del Grimsby

Well there's no need to be so depressing about it, there's a positive side too – Britain's going to get warmer and sunnier. Hoorah!

I do lots of other things for the environment

I already do loads. I recycle my bottles, use the bus, re-use my plastic bags, sponsor a donkey.

I will if everyone else does

This is very important and I intend to take it very seriously, but I think I'll wait until everyone else does first.

It's not me

I'm not the problem. It's the Americans, Chinese, corporations, rich people, people with the stupid big cars that take up all the parking spaces. Come to think of it, I think it's *you*, Mr. Eco Smartypants.

Be honest, some of these registered with you, didn't they? There is nothing wrong with that. Although some of them are a bit defensive and some a bit offensive, all are legitimate, personal responses to the problem. Most people *do* feel overwhelmed by day-to-day life. As individuals we are only a very small part of the overall problem. It *is* true that there are other huge problems in the world, and it *is* also true that there are positive signs of change.

And, as we discuss in the next section, you may decide, after weighing everything up, that your best personal strategy on climate change will be to do nothing. However, we are not talking at all yet about what you can do, and, although these arguments appear to be concerned with action, in reality they are designed to provide reasons for *not listening*, for blocking out all of the incoming information about the problem, and for saying, 'Oh yes, yes I know all about that, but . . . '. They are not the conclusion of any thought, but the justification for not thinking.

Chapter 8

Comedy corner
It's talent night at the Sceptic Social Club

Let's just sum up with a diatribe that neatly brings together every denial strategy we've talked about so far.

'I don't think the advice of a bunch of UN scientists should be taken as gospel truth. Human breathing is one of the biggest problems as far as I can see, so why don't these hairy environmentalists just shoot all the humans.

'The environmentalists are like the CND nutters in the 1970s. They banged on about being against nuclear war, but you can't change the world by putting on a pair of dungarees or sandals. I listen to all this drivel about turning down the central heating, going back to candles, returning to the dark ages. You do that if you want to. But none of it will make any difference. It just panders to your middle-class, middle-aged angst and guilt.

'Climate change is just politicians pandering to the latest fashion. Taxes on fuel are all just stealth taxes. It is just another way of stealing things from hard-pressed consumers. It's like parking tickets and congestion charging.

'Gordon Brown wants us all to believe that he spends his days mulching his compost with his children, but he still

121

rushes round his constituency in an SUV with a fleet of secret service cars at weekends. There should be a tax on the Chancellor.

'It's the Russians, the Chinese and the Indians we have to influence. They keep opening more and more coal- and oil-fired power stations. Soon it won't matter how many lights we turn off nor how many bicycles we ride nor how many flights we make, the damage will have been done on the other side of the world by a billion other people.'

Can you see who it is yet? Step forward Michael O'Leary, head of cut-price airline Ryanair.

Chapter 9

Climate change – bring it on!

Why some people can't wait for Costa Del Grimsby

So this is how the logic goes. Yes, climate change is happening – we'd be stupid not to believe all the boffins – but we don't have to believe their scare stories about how bad it will be. It could be great, especially in cold and grey Britain.

This cheery version of climate change is particularly appealing to Winners, whose spiritual home is California. Newspapers run this story with infuriating regularity. Here's a typical example from the *Daily Express* on 5 June 2004:

'British summers will become as hot as Australia by 2100. By 2100 future generations will enjoy Sydney-style barbecue weather for more than a fifth of the year with temperatures ranging from 26 to 29°C (79-84°F). A spokesman for the Australian High Commission warned: "The temperatures will be hard on traditional ale drinkers. You might need to go over to coolers full of tinnies. But then again you might just win the Rugby World Cup again."'

Well, ho, ho, ho

It raises a question that you should always ask when you hear this kind of thing. If Britain really is going to be like Sydney in summer (and don't forget that means flash flooding and hurricane-force winds in winter), then what the hell is Sydney going to be like?

In January 2001, during the worst drought in a thousand years, Australian government scientists predicted that by 2070 – that is still 30 years short of 2100 – Sydney would have severe droughts for nine years out of ten and will have to recycle treated sewage into the domestic water supply. They predicted that summer temperatures in Sydney's suburbs could rise by as much as 7° to 42°C (108°F), leading to an extra 1,300 deaths each year from heatstroke.

So this is the great greenhouse future for Australians: huddled around the air conditioner drinking their own pee

Here's another example that keeps appearing – the old chestnut about vineyards in Surrey. A witty wine column called Vino Veritas puts it this way:

'Global warming might be the slow drip-feed of death to the planet, but to the wine drinker it has its upsides . . . we will have an English wine industry again.'

Vino Veritas is the in-house wine column of *Lloyds List*, the leading publication of the British insurance industry. With climate-related claims set to treble by 2050, climate change has the potential to bankrupt the insurance industry, which might explain the strong desire to open another bottle and not think too much about it.

Once again, the question you should be asking is, 'If we will be able to grow wine in England, what are they going to be growing in the existing wine-growing areas?'

The French and Italian wine industries are in an increasing panic because it is clear that, within fifty years, the current varieties will no longer be able to be grow in their traditional areas. A recent report by the Commonwealth Scientific and Research Organization (CSIRO), the main Australian scientific research organization, argued that temperature increases by 2030 would reduce Australian grape quality by over 50 per cent. Great news for wine drinkers.

But I will stop there because I'm starting to peep too closely at that climate Medusa again. Just take it as read that there are no winners in this game.

Chapter 10

The plastic bag fetish

How we glorify trivial actions to make it look as if we are doing something

In a town near me a small group of dedicated teenagers formed a climate-change action group. But their first meeting ground to a standstill because one person – a local Tory councillor, as it happens – insisted that she knew the answer. 'Plastic bags. We *must* recycle the plastic bags.' She was nicknamed the Bag Lady.

The truth is that there may be lots of good reasons for recycling your plastic bags – they are ugly, wasteful rubbish that fouls up the countryside, rivers and oceans – but they make doodly squat difference to climate change. An average plastic bag produces 31 grammes of carbon dioxide, about the same as comes from driving my car 90 metres (300 feet). That doesn't get me very far towards the supermarket. If I was in a jetplane it wouldn't get me to the end of my garden.

Once put within the context of our overall emissions, plastic bags are virtually irrelevant – accounting for just 5 kilogrammes of the 12½ *tonnes* of carbon dioxide the average Brit puts out per year. That is scarcely 36 seconds of our total daily emissions.

I'm sorry to tell you, but adopting some diversionary good behaviour is a classic psychological strategy of people who don't want to face up to facts. In the case of climate change, this innate tendency is actively encouraged by all those articles that outline some catastrophic climate impacts and then provide a box of 'small easy things you can do now to make a difference'. As we found in Part 1, putting the two together just causes confusion and cynicism (see pages 26–7).

Supermarkets are keen to play to people's desire for bite-sized solutions. They provide plastic-bag recycling bins or offer you special 'eco' bags that you can re-use. Tesco is running a scheme for people to recycle their Christmas cards. Well, thank heavens. I'm sure the orang-utans can sleep easier at night now.

Organizations are also prone to absurd token activity. Here are my three all time favourites.

• In third place is the self-styled 'greenest petrol station in the world' in Essex, which BP unveiled with much hoo-hah in 2001. Solar panels and wind turbines on the roof power the lights and petrol pumps.

• In the number two slot are the three windmills that power the Ford diesel-engine plant in Dagenham.

• And the winner. In 2006 Virgin Airlines announced the first step towards reducing the climate impacts of their transatlantic flights: they will plant trees to soak up the emissions of the limousines that pick up their first-class air passengers.

These are extreme and laughable examples of the token gestures made by highly polluting industries – and there are many more. Although they smell like cynical publicity stunts, I suspect that the real intended audience is the company's own employees. Even if people don't love their employers, they still want to believe that their work is worthwhile and making a positive contribution to the world. Don't we all?

The lesson is that you need to keep everything in perspective. There are strong and accurate objective measures of our climate impacts and it is these that should guide our actions. As we discover in the next section, the only thing that really counts is the carbon bottom line. And I have a great new marketing idea for the supermarkets. Air miles for plastic bags. If you save ten bags you get one free air mile. That way you can 'save the planet', 'make a difference' and have fun. A win-win for everyone.

Chapter 11

Hiding in the crowd

Why we are conditioned to wait for someone else to do something

I expect you have heard of the frog-in-a-pot. If you put a frog in a saucepan of cold water and slowly increase the temperature, it will slowly cook to death because the temperature rises too slowly to alert it to the danger.

It is a nice image for our own failure to deal with incremental problems like climate change and is one used by Sir David King, the chief scientific advisor to the government. Unfortunately, according to the sadistic experimenters who have tried it, it is not true. Frogs are smarter than this and hop out as soon as it gets too warm. It's still a great story, and I don't suppose that urban myths need be subjected to verification and peer review.

Here is a better metaphor that really is true. If you put caterpillars on the rim of a teacup they will follow each other round and round until they drop off from exhaustion. There are plenty of reasons why they wouldn't want to get off the rim – it's a long way down after all with a big lake of tea on one side – so they are only too happy to follow the caterpillar in front in the hope that it has a better idea of what to do.

And here we are with climate change, following each other's green hairy bottoms

Nothing to do with me, guv

My father liked to tell this story. One day he was on his way to work on the London Underground. There was a mad woman who, while muttering and shouting abuse, was picking up all the rubbish and making a large pile at one end of the carriage. Then she got out the matches. My father was the shyest man you could imagine – hardly one to put himself forward – but he was certain that, had he not intervened, *no one* else would have done anything.

This is a good example of a phenomenon that psychologists call the 'bystander effect'. The principle is quite simple. Whenever there are other people around we have a ready excuse for holding back and waiting to see what they do. 'After all,' we reckon, 'why should *I* be the person to become involved? Maybe I am misjudging what is going on. Maybe someone else is about to sort it out.'

The problem is that everyone else in the crowd is making the same calculation. The more people that are present, the greater the diffusion of responsibility and the less the chance that anyone at all will step forward. Attacks, rapes and even murders happen in crowded places in broad daylight. Newspapers run despairing editorials deploring the decline of community spirit, but there is really nothing new in this at all. It is just the bystander effect.

Now consider climate change. We can all see the

problem, but we are all standing around, watching and waiting to see what anyone else does. 'After all,' we reckon, 'why should *I* be the person to become involved? Maybe I have got it wrong. Maybe someone else will sort it out.' And when we look at the other people they are giving us no indication that there is any problem at all – they are still flying round and burning up oil as fast as they can.

There is a lot of finger-pointing when it comes to climate change – it's the business of the government, the corporations, the United Nations. It is as though we are in a large crowd standing around someone being mugged and complaining loudly about how long it is taking for the police to arrive.

However, for once there is good news. In experiments, psychologists found that people who knew about the bystander effect were ten times more likely to intervene in a staged crime. A week after I first heard about the effect, I was in a full cinema when the film snapped. But I had been cured and I found the projectionist outside having a cigarette. When I went back in, the entire audience was still sitting there, staring at a blank screen, wondering when the hell someone would do something.

Now that you know about the effect, you will never again *assume* that anyone in a large crowd will do anything. That does not mean that you will necessarily do something yourself. But it does mean that you are much more likely to take your own initiative rather than wait for someone else to break ranks. And you now know that, just because other people are not doing anything, it does not mean that what it happening is not important.

Chapter 12

Meet your Evil Carbon Twin

Why we believe that our actions will be undone by someone else

Last year I dropped in on my neighbour to settle some minor boundary dispute. There was a walloping four-wheel-drive tank in his drive; his house was as hot as a sauna with the back door open; every room was lit up like an operating theatre by halogen spots and a 1.8 metre (6 foot) wide plasma-screen TV was going full throttle in the corner with no one paying any attention to it.

Now I live a very low-carbon lifestyle. I cycle to work, rarely if ever fly, and have done everything I can to reduce the energy consumption of my house. As soon as I saw his house I realized: all the energy that my own energy-efficient house and low-impact living was saving was being used up by *him*. I was turning down my thermostat 2° so that he could turn his up. I was cycling to work so that he could have more road space for his Land Cruiser. I was turning everything off so that he could leave it on all day.

I might just as well have run a cable between our houses and sent all the energy that I was saving straight over to him.

I'd met my Evil Carbon Twin.

Fantasy stories often have the idea of the evil doppelgänger who sets you up and undoes everything you do. There is *Dead Ringer* with Bette Davis and *The Dark Mirror* with Olivia de Haviland. In *Friends* Phoebe Buffay has an evil twin named Ursula. Even Bart Simpson has an evil twin Hugo.

The Evil Carbon Twin is probably the single greatest impediment to personal action on climate change. Even people who are passionate about the threat of climate change are often paralysed by the thought that someone else could undo their own actions.

Sometimes this twin is someone we know with a cheap-flight habit. Sometimes the twin is more abstract – someone rich, someone with a big flash car. And sometimes the twin is living in another country with loads of children.

Something interesting to note about these twins: they invariably reflect long-standing political or cultural prejudices. Strivers and Winners blame each other. Traditionalists blame Survivors. Everyone blames Americans, who, as we know, all drive stupidly big cars. Talk to Americans, and you find that their evil twins live in China. The US Senate has even passed a law, called the

Byrd-Hagel Resolution, which says that it will refuse to ratify any international climate treaty that does not also 'mandate scheduled commitments from Developing Country Parties'. Well, we know that's code for the Chinese.

And what do the Chinese say? When challenged about their own emissions they say that before they will do anything, they want to see significant action by the people who released the greenhouse gases that are already in the atmosphere. Seeing that we started the industrial revolution, that means *us*.

And so it all goes round and round in the international brotherhood of finger-pointing. In all cases the argument is the same – there is no point doing anything unless we do something about my neighbour, my Uncle Sid, the Americans, Chinese, Chinese-Americans, poor people, rich people, people with lots of kids.

In fact, now that you know that your twins and their progeny are lurking out there somewhere, why should you even bother starting? You'll only find out sooner or later how pointless it all is.

Let's deal with this argument stage by stage

The reason that the Evil Carbon Twin is so powerful is that we are constantly being told that we have a moral responsibility to make personal sacrifices to reduce a huge global problem – to 'do our bit' to 'save the planet'.

But this is a very poor reason to reduce emissions. Of course, we feel utterly dispirited when we see that there are all these freeloaders who are not only refusing to 'do their bit' but are using up what we save. It feels like putting money into a charity appeals box and then seeing the tin shakers later that evening spending it all in the pub.

So forget this argument, because it doesn't work.

Stop thinking about climate change as something you have to give up. Stop thinking that you, little you, are going to 'save the planet'

The real reason you should reduce your own emissions is because you *want* to live differently. When you detox you will do it as a statement of who you are – a smart and aware person living in the 21st century. OK, so my neighbour is still living in the 20th century. Well that's his problem, and it's all going to catch up with him in the end (see Say no to sackcloth, pages 161–3).

Now that you know the damage your emissions cause you don't want to be a part of it, regardless of what anyone else may do. It is just like any other ethical issue. You don't whip your children or mug pensioners or burn down schools or steal cars or kick dogs because you believe those things are wrong and doing them would undermine your opinion of yourself as a good person. Whether your neighbour or anyone in China does these things is a matter for concern, but provides no excuse for you not to do them. The fact that people in the 20th century used to beat their children regularly is no reason you would want to do it in the 21st.

People often do damaging things through ignorance. My neighbour hasn't yet recognized the damage caused by his emissions. That doesn't make him a bad person – in fact he's a very nice fellow. But ignorance doesn't defend something that is wrong. And you are much smarter than that.

Let's look at China

Each Chinese person produces an average of 5 tonnes of carbon dioxide (and equivalent gases) per year. That's less than half our average emissions, and much of it comes from the factories producing consumer goods for our market. That's hardly stealing our sweets. Could not a Chinese person be far more justified in seeing a Brit as his Evil Carbon Twin.

We fixate on the Chinese because we have a historical fear of the 'faceless' Asian hordes. Do you remember that old myth about how all the Chinese could jump up and down and create a tidal wave that would wipe out California? Isn't it interesting that the threat to America came from *West* not the East? The assumption was that a billion brainwashed Chinese could be corralled into this act of aggression. Peace-loving Europeans would never mobilize en masse to attack people. Oh no.

And no one mentioned that if the force of all those jumping Chinese really was strong enough to create a huge tidal wave, it would also be strong enough to wipe out every Chinese city

These days we regularly hear that a mass jump in Chinese living standards will create a climate tsunami. China, we hear, is building a coal-fired power station every five days. China, we hear, has the fastest-growing car market in the world. 'God help us,' say the commentators, 'if all those Chinese get air conditioning.' All true. But it is also true that, like the mass jump, the impacts of climate change will probably be greater for them than for us. They may be locked into the same self-destructive path as the rest of us, but this is not some piece of selfish aggression on their part.

Why not challenge your Evil Carbon Twin?

Finally, let's turn the whole argument on its head. The Evil Carbon Twin is not an argument for giving up at all: it's a powerful argument for doing the exact opposite. If you really believe that other people – be they rich people, Chinese, Americans or your neighbour – were the main cause of an urgent and appalling crisis then you would be doing something to tackle them and change their behaviour. After all, as you now know, we are very energized by problems when the enemy is one against whom we can mobilize (see pages 93–4).

As soon as you start to think about it, there are virtually unlimited things you could be doing. Here is a short list of strategies to deal with your Evil Carbon Twins:

• Put your savings somewhere that does not invest in China or oil companies.

• Distribute energy-saving leaflets in your neighbourhood.

• Raise the issue of climate change at work and persuade your employer and work colleagues to take collective action.

• Support organizations that campaign for political and social change wherever you think is the main habitat for your Twins (the US, China and so on).

• Take your Uncle Sid on one side and tell him why you think that his RangeRover/holiday in Florida/second home in Spain is not such a great idea.

● Even better, start to turn your Uncle Sid into a Low Carbon Twin by working with him to insulate his house (see Get a carbon buddy pages 277–8).

At the very least, you could write to your MP and say that you want him or her to take climate change seriously and demand diplomatic pressure or the withdrawal of investments from/higher taxes for China/the US/rich people/corporations/Uncle Sid/the bloke who lives next door (delete where applicable).

Have you done anything like this? It all sounds a bit worthy and eco-activist doesn't it? And, of course, it does, because we know that the people who are doing these things are the ones who *have* also changed their lightbulbs and are thinking long and hard about their flying. The people who really take action against their Evil Carbon Twins are also those doing everything they can to sort out their own responsibility because they know that what they do should dance with what they believe (see Five great reasons for detoxing, pages 164–71, and Your actions and your principles will dance together, page 166.

So the real reason why the Evil Carbon Twin argument seems attractive is that it provides an excuse for not *believing* in the problem. This is a variation on the bystander effect, whereby we avoid becoming involved by saying to ourselves: 'It's their problem: they are causing it so they can sort it out.'

Part 5
Strategies for dealing with climate change

Chapter 1

The five strategies for personal engagement with climate change

Make your choice

I have looked at this from every angle, and I still come down to the same conclusion: anything that you do about climate change is a variation on just five basic strategies.

1 Do nothing. Decide to ignore it and hope that someone else does something.

2 Adapt. Recognize that climate change is happening and plan your life around its impacts.

3 Carbon detox. Embrace the challenge of low-carbon living. Decide that you are a smart 21st-century person who lives differently and reduce your emissions.

4 Thrive. Realize the personal opportunities that climate change will bring for people who are canny and ahead of the curve.

5 Take control. Decide that you do not want passively to accept the problem and that you want to use your influence to prevent it.

In this chapter I will look at just the first two of these options – they are short and easily dealt with. The rest of the book is given over to he remaining three options, especially the carbon detox, which I believe is the foundation to any effective action on climate change.

So think long and hard – *what* are you going to do?

Strategy 1: Do nothing

You cannot ignore climate change. It is real, true and, if you ignore it, you are due for a very rude awakening. So you must accept and believe that climate change is happening and that it will have major impacts on your future. To ignore the truth is to live a lie and to deceive yourself.

If you do accept it, then you may still decide that there is nothing at all that you can do. You may feel that the problem is too large, that you are too powerless or that there is no point. You may be able to sit it out for a few more years yet, but very soon no one will be allowed to do nothing. The real choice is between doing something yourself now and preparing yourself for the huge changes that are coming or waiting until someone else imposes their agenda on you.

Strategy 2: Adapt

If you believe in climate change and accept that it is a major issue during your lifetime, the least you can do is to be ready for it. You will be prepared mentally for changes. You do not know exactly what they will be, or when they will come, but, like the twists on the rollercoaster, you know that there are some coming, including nasty surprises, and when they come you recognize that they were due. Even if you are a Survivor, living from day to day, this is the most basic strategy to keep your life on an even keel.

Adapting makes you a conscious passenger on the climate rollercoaster. You are well belted in and, like a good scout, you are *never* unprepared for whatever is coming along. There are two components to an adaptation strategy.

Be prepared for the direct impacts of climate change

You should evaluate all your present and future decisions in the light of climate change and its likely impacts. Being smart is knowing the right questions, and in this case the smart question is: how will climate change affect this?

Think carefully about where you choose to live. This is not a good time to own a house in any area that is subject to flooding, whether from rivers, drainage culverts or the sea. Research carefully into the potential local climate change impacts when buying any property on a floodplain or close to the sea. In some cases, houses in flood-risk areas could become impossible to insure or even to sell, so it is clearly smart to get out of these areas before you lose the value of your house. You might also want to think carefully before buying a house in an exposed wind-vulnerable or coastal location.

The Environment Agency has a very detailed online map that tells you which areas are currently subject to a 1-in-100-year risk of flooding and a 1-in-1,000-year risk of flooding. What this map does not tell you is how climate change will affect these risks.

This is where the gamble comes. Department for the Environment (DEFRA) research shows a very wide range of risks of flooding by 2080. The current costs of flooding are around £2 billion a year. If we are lucky – that is, if emissions stabilize at a safe level and if the government follows the optimal strategy – the impacts of flooding may increase by just £1 billion. However, if emissions continue to soar and the government messes it all up, flood damage could increase tenfold to £27 billion a year by 2080. There are many contingencies in here, but personally I would not be keen to put any money on the most optimistic scenario.

What the research also shows is a dramatic increase in urban flash flooding because sewers and drainage systems will not be able to deal with the sudden downpours predicted under climate change. Under all options the number of properties at risk will more than treble by 2080. This sounds a long time away, but the research suggests that most of these increases will be manifested by 2050. And we are already well on the way. The disastrous flooding of July 2007 is set to cost £6 billion. Seven years earlier in Autumn 2000 the heaviest rains ever recorded in the UK led to £1.3 billion in insurance claims.

Heatwaves will also play a significant role in future summers and could be a serious danger to old people, and extra insulation could well be more important for keeping the heat out than keeping the heat in. You could also plant trees to the south of the house that can shade the house during the peak of summer and drop their leaves in winter to let through the low winter sun.

Some businesses may be substantially affected by climate change and the impacts of extreme weather events. Insurance, farming and fisheries will be hit the hardest, and there may also be significant impacts on tourism, construction and all activities conducted outdoors. Consider any potential impacts from climate change on your career and investment choices. In some of these areas, especially farming and tourism, the climatic changes will also bring new opportunities, so you should also consider whether climate change might influence your strategy and require a shift in priorities. People who choose to 'thrive' will be doing precisely this.

Please note this: it is extremely unwise to purchase a holiday home or plan to retire to a hotter climate without getting the best advice you can on the future impacts of climate change in that region. You should absolutely avoid the assumption that because everyone else seems to be investing in an area, there is no problem. I can guarantee that very few of these other people will have given a moment's thought to the future impacts of climate change.

Take Spain, for example. According to all of the models, Spain will be the European country most affected by climate change, with summer temperatures expected to increase by up to 6°C (11°F) by 2100. In the south this will be combined with a 40 per cent decline in rainfall. Arturo Gonzalo Aizpiri, the senior advisor on climate change for the Spanish environment ministry, says: 'Everybody should be worried because the heatwaves are going to become more and more frequent, beaches are disappearing, tropical diseases are appearing in Spain and anyone who has contact with the countryside has noticed the disappearance of species.' By the estimates of his own ministry, 90 per cent of the southern region is now at risk of desertification as the North African desert leapfrogs across the Mediterranean.

Spain is seeing a rapid increase in the demand for water from agriculture, tourism and new housing at the same time as an alarming decline in rainfall. In 2006, during the worst drought in 60 years, 1.5 million new homes were built in Spain – 40 per cent of all the housing construction in Europe. Personally, I consider it utter folly to buy one of them without seriously considering future climate impacts.

And that is not all. In 2006 the first ever hurricane to hit Europe landed on the northwestern coast of Spain.

Scientists had previously thought it impossible for a hurricane to form in the northern Atlantic but with climate change all bets are off.

Be prepared for the political responses to climate change

The UK government is committed to a 60 per cent reduction in emissions by 2050. Although we have achieved a 15 per cent fall in emissions since 1990, this was almost entirely owing to the shift from coal to gas generation in electricity power stations and the decline in heavy industry. Future reductions will be harder to achieve and will require far deeper changes in our lives.

Of course, as we all know, governments are always coming up with daft targets that sound good in a press release but will never be achieved. So you can take a gamble that the government will fudge this, just the same as it has fudged its targets on child poverty, overseas development, traffic congestion and so on.

I believe, though, that this particular target needs to be taken far more seriously. For one thing, it has an unprecedented cross-party endorsement, which means it will not be dropped if the government changes. For another, it has been the basis of a pan-European target to hit a 20 per cent reduction by 2030, which will set up external pressure for compliance (and competition from other countries). It has also inspired California to go one step further and aim for an 80 per cent cut by 2050 – who would ever have thought that Arnold Schwartzenegger would come up with that?

And finally, given the trajectory of climate change and the clear evidence of its

acceleration, political pressure can only mount. This issue will not go away

So far the government has been very unwilling to tackle personal lifestyle choices. Yet, with the rising transport and household-energy consumption threatening to undo all of the gains of the past ten years, it will be impossible for future governments to avoid direct intervention in public behaviour – and that means *your* behaviour.

All political parties are considering the same limited range of policies – they can tax fuel, legislate for energy efficiency, subsidize energy conservation and renewables, ration fuel consumption or enable emissions trading. All of these policies depend on the same basic pincer movement: charging the high emitters and using the proceeds to reward the low emitters.

Being prepared for climate change therefore requires recognizing the fact that there will be strong penalties for high-emissions lifestyles.

In the 2006 budget Gordon Brown put a £210 surcharge on the road tax for high fuel consuming cars. In 2007 he increased that to £400. Of course, this is no real disincentive for people who can fork out £30,000 or more for a car and pay over the odds to run it. But it signals a long-term policy of taxing cars on the basis of fuel consumption. It is very rare for new taxes to be reduced or removed, and I safely predict that this is a tax that will increase substantially.

And then there is housing. I can see no way that the government can ever achieve the 60 per cent target without substantial penalties for the people who live in inefficient houses and rewards for those living in efficient ones. From 2008 anyone selling a house will need to prepare an independent energy audit. To begin with this audit will inform the choices of house buyers, but it would be only a small step for it to become the basis of council tax bands, and only a small step from there for minimum standards to be required before a house can be sold at all.

In 2004 the University of Oxford was commissioned to look in detail at the housing sector and identify how, in practical terms, it could meet the target of a 60 per cent reduction in emissions within 50 years. It concluded that the 60 per cent target could be reached provided that *every* house in the country was insulated to the highest possible standard and fitted with solar-power generation and provided that 3 million of the worst efficiency houses were demolished and replaced.

That means that every house in Britain will face mandatory renovation with costs proportional to the size and age of the house, and that these costs will be reflected in the market value of houses

Unlike cars or refrigerators, houses are long-term investments. Although policy in this area is still moving slowly and concentrating on new buildings, the government will soon have to decide a long-term policy for reducing emissions from the existing housing stock. And if you don't believe that the government will ever legislate in the way I suggested, you have to ask: how else they will ever reach the emissions target?

All in all, given the direction of future policy, if you were buying a house you would be wise to make the energy performance of the house as great a consideration as its appearance and location.

And finally, there is the issue of flights. The government is predicting that air travel in and out of the UK will double by 2030. As many people have pointed out, not least the Met Office's own Hadley Centre for Climate Prediction and Research, if this happens the growth in emissions from flights will swamp all other policies to reduce emissions.

So once again, I ask you. If you were in a government of any political stripe, trying to meet a very tight emissions target, would you allow one area receiving huge tax subsidies to expand without control and destroy your chances of meeting that target?

A range of policies is being considered in the UK and EU to curtail the growth in aviation and they will all increase the costs for flying: a single 'green' passenger tax; higher landing charges or restrictions on the number of landing slots; and emissions trading, which will also come in the form of a carbon tax on airlines.

I am unconvinced that any of the current policies will significantly curtail people's demand for flights, never mind reducing them in line with the 60 per cent target. Flying is currently far cheaper than public transport by land because there is no VAT on flight tickets and there is no tax on aviation fuel. Shifting travel back to land transport will need to reverse these tax breaks, and this could mean trebling the cost of a flight.

More than 2 million Britons already own a home abroad, and that figure is expected to double over the next ten years. Many of these are retirement homes – according to government figures one million British pensioners are drawing their state pension abroad and 800,000 of them are second homes. In both cases people's dreams and financial security are inextricably bound to the belief that cheap flights are a permanent feature of the modern world. This is very unlikely to be the case, and I argue strongly that this is a very risky assumption on which to base major decisions and invest life savings.

Being prepared is the first step to getting real about climate change. But it is still passive. Adapters may be able to sit out the storm, but they are doing little to prevent the next one. There are huge changes coming in social attitudes, government policy and lifestyles. Adapters will constantly be at the back of the pack, struggling to keep up. The people who will be setting the pace will be those who are demanding change, engaging with their own emissions and taking advantage of the new opportunities. The rest of this book is dedicated to them.

Part 6
The vision

Chapter 1

The vision

How things could be

When you decide to detox you are not just taking a stand *against* climate change. You are also making a strong statement *for* a cleaner, healthier and fairer world. This is what it could be like.

Imagine that you live in a place that you can feel proud of and really call home. A place that is special and unlike anywhere else. Where you know everyone on your street and where friends are always close to hand.

Imagine that your house is comfortable all year round. In winter it is cosy and warm. In summer it is cool and fresh. Your house generates all of its own power and you never have to pay a fuel bill.

Imagine the street belongs to people again. There are children playing in the road. People are sitting in the sun, walking and cycling, or just standing in the middle of the road chatting.

Imagine that when you step out of your front door the air is always clean and fresh. You are fit and thin and feeling great – getting lots of rejuvenating exercise and eating a great diet.

Imagine that there is plenty of work for everyone near where they live.

Imagine that you never have to commute to work again.

Never have to sit in a traffic jam. Never have to fight over a parking space. Everything that you need and everyone that you want to see is a short walk or cycle ride away.

Imagine that the only things you own are the things that you really love and value. You don't have to spend months every year working for things you don't need or for a car or a holiday or to pay the fuel bills.

Imagine that this gives you the freedom to work less and spend more time with friends and family or to do something you really want to do.

Imagine that travelling is a real adventure again, that the journey itself is a thrill and that every destination has its own unique character.

Imagine that people feel the need to go to places only when they have a really good reason and that when they get there they are welcomed as honoured guests.

Imagine a world where the wonders of technology – the medicine, surgery, lights, video computers, electronic magic, the excitements of speed, power and noise – are something rare and special that are savoured, valued and never taken for granted.

Imagine a world where people of all politics, classes and cultures can put their differences aside and unite around a common cause.

Imagine that through this unity of purpose we can concentrate on ensuring that everyone has the same rights to a basic standard of health and living.

   And finally:

Imagine that this is not just a standard of living for wealthy countries like Britain, but a standard to which all the peoples of the world are entitled to aspire and are helped to achieve.

This is not some personal fantasy

Everything in this vision follows directly from the measures needed to deal with climate change.

The changes to our homes, streets and travel all derive from the reduction of home and transport emissions.

The reduction of uncessessary transport would lead to the greater localization of production and services and more local jobs. The Oxford University Environmental Change Institute calculates that the need to refurbish half a million homes a year will create a huge boost to local economies and will create 50,000 permanent new jobs, many of them in the most deprived areas of the country. And this is just one aspect of the new economy.

The end of energy-intensive agriculture will incentivize the production of seasonal organic produce and will discourage the excessive consumption of meat and processed foods. The diet that results from these measures is strongly recommended by dieticians as optimal for health.

In the present high-emission economy the structure of day-to-day life is based around the struggle to maintain a high level of mobility and consumption. At present few people have the option of downsizing or working less. The changes we need to make should make it possible for many more people to opt for a simpler lifestyle – especially those who want to live without a car, which, after housing, is the single largest item of spending. And the very high cost of housing, which is a huge source of stress for working people, could be far more affordable if we used the existing housing better with higher occupancy and no second homes – both measures required to deal with climate change.

I am confident that measures to reduce emissions will create a more just society. I don't think that voters will ever support a government that reduces emissions by making fuel and petrol extremely expensive, but I do think that voters might support a policy based on carbon rationing and trading. If people want to go over their ration by flying or driving a fancy car they will have to buy emissions from someone who is living simply. For the first time in human history, the rich will have to buy their lifestyles from the poor. It's not socialism, but it is a powerful form of redistributive justice that has fans among the left and the right. And I believe it will work.

There is a proposal for a similar mechanism at an international scale called Contraction and Convergence, which would give everyone in the world the same carbon allowance and would force rich countries either to reduce their emissions or buy spare rations from the poor countries. This model has plenty of weaknesses, but it has one major strength: a single set of rules applies to everyone based around a right to an equal share of the atmosphere. Contraction and Convergence is far from being a fringe proposal – it has some powerful supporters, including national governments.

However, I run a risk here of getting off topic. I do not want to discuss specific proposals for a low-carbon economy. There are many excellent books that discuss this. Instead I want to make a much simpler point.

It is hard to be motivated by dread or excited about something when we feel forced to do it. But we can feel excited about the carbon detox if we recognize that it leads the way to a world that could be better for everyone. Climate change is not all bad news – it could be the catalyst for a positive transformation in our society that might otherwise never have happened. When we decide to detox we are becoming an active part of a much larger movement.

Part 7
Preparing for the detox

Chapter 1

The carbon detox
Why you will want to do it

Carbon, that black, grubby element that loves to combine with other elements, is the main element in fossil fuels like coal and oil. When you burn them the carbon joins up with oxygen to make carbon dioxide. I'm sure I could tell you more about it if I hadn't been doodling fighter planes through double chemistry.

All living things contain carbon compounds and when they die and rot their carbon is released to produce more carbon dioxide or, if there isn't enough oxygen around, an even more powerful greenhouse gas – methane.

This should all be in balance. The released carbon should all be mopped up by forests and oceans, but the problem, as we now know, is that we have spent the last five hundred years tracking down the deposits of carbon that were permanently removed and locked up in the form of oil, coal and peat deposits and burning them. The newly liberated carbon has teamed up with its old partner oxygen and is swamping all of the natural removal systems. Each year we add 21 billion tonnes more carbon dioxide to the air than these systems can remove.

So we have managed to turn this useful and important

element into a menace. We have to stop digging it up and we have to find ways of living without burning it. We have to de-carbonize.

However, I don't feel excited when people say that we will have to move to a low-carbon economy or that we will have to adopt low-carbon lifestyles. 'Low' things are not inspiring – they smell of giving things up. If 'high living' sounds like a skyscraper penthouse, then 'low living' sounds like a damp bedsit in the basement. These are useful terms and I sometimes use them myself, but I think we need to find some different terms to describe this if we want to be inspired.

A new way of thinking

I want you to think of all that carbon as a weight. Each Briton is responsible for digging up and burning $3\frac{1}{2}$ tonnes of carbon each year, which when it combines with oxygen, makes $12\frac{1}{2}$ tonnes of carbon dioxide. Think of it as a huge load on your shoulders that doesn't just threaten your future but ties you down and chains you to the ground. Instead of reducing it or giving it up, I'd like you to think of dropping that load. I would like you to aspire to **light living** – a lifestyle without that heavy load of carbon.

• **Light** in the sense of floating free of all that stuff that holds us down; being light on our feet, fit, mobile and agile.

• **Light** in the sense of treading lightly on the earth, dancing not stomping.

• **Light** in the sense of embracing all the power of the sunshine.

- **Light** in the sense of brightness and freshness – letting light and air into our lives.

Light living recognizes and incorporates climate change into our lives in a way that is positive, constructive and smart. It is a richer, fuller and healthier way of living that keeps our personal emissions within the capacity of the planet. Many of the things that cause climate change are related to shutting ourselves away in our boxes with our artificial light and our stifling heating or our freezing air conditioning. So open up the windows, pull back the curtains and let daylight and fresh air flood into your life.

The way you will be able to achieve that lighter life is to *detox*, to let go of that filthy, sooty stuff that blackens the air, clogs up your lungs and blocks out the sun. You need to clean up your life and drop the load so that you can float free.

The rest of this book shows how you can change and seek out the parts of your life that are loaded down with carbon. You will discover how to develop an action plan and choose your priorities, and, in just one year, you will drop at least one tonne. Won't that be a weight off your shoulders?

Chapter 2

Say no to sackcloth

Why dropping the carbon is not a penance

First of all, let's be clear – light living is not about becoming a climate saint: it is about doing things differently.

So, let's get rid of some ideas. You are not adopting an 'alternative lifestyle'. That suggests that you are joining some kind of parallel universe or cult. As we already know, labels are dangerous, so let's get rid of some of those. You are not about to become a greenie or an eco or a crusty or a crumbly or a swampy or anything you don't want to be. All you are going to do is live in the modern world.

You are not 'saving the planet'

I want to say this to everyone, including the most dedicated greens: **'Please don't do this to 'save the planet'**. Of course, your actions are important and contribute to the huge shift we will all make. You will be a positive role model for everyone around you. Your purchases will send a signal through the markets to change production. You will be helping to make that vision of a new world real.

But you need to do it for the right reasons. If you are changing the way you live out of guilt or fear, then you are setting yourself up for a fall and positively inviting an encounter with your Evil Carbon Twin. You should not see the detox as a rearguard action to hold back the tidal wave. You are choosing to live lighter as a statement that you are a smart 21st-century person who wants to be a part of a new way of living.

You are not going to give anything up.

Everyone hates having things taken away – it feels like having our toys confiscated. So this is not a loss, it's a gain. As we detox, we are not going to give anything up: we are going to do things differently. We are going to holiday differently, travel differently, work differently and live differently.

Just think how differently we live now compared to a hundred years ago. Think of the middle-class Victorian home with all those drapes and festoons, tassels and knick-knacks, stuffed birds and whatnots and buttoned velvet pouffes. Even the richest people now live in houses that would seem like extreme monastic poverty to Victorians. Imagine suggesting to a Victorian that he could be happier with fewer things. He would be horrified. 'What! You want me to *give up* my rococo gilt ormolu-mounted wax-fruit pedestal? Egad sir, how dare you?!'

And yet we have happily adjusted to living in far simpler ways. We don't live *worse*, we live *differently*. For a hundred years smart, progressive, modern people have lived lighter, and we have followed them.

Now, with the benefit of hindsight, we also recognize the gross injustice of Victorian society where some people were living with huge piles of useless stuff and others were dying in the workhouse. I'm afraid that in a hundred years people will be making a similar observation about the impact that our emissions are having on the people in the Third World.

Of course, there are always those Evil Carbon Twins out there. You may well ask, 'Why should I bother to live differently when everyone else can still keep living the same way?' And I'd say that the question is still hooked onto this idea of giving something up. It is asking, 'Why should I give up my toys when my twin doesn't have to?' And the answer is the same: you are not giving something up. You are dropping it so that you can live differently and because it makes sense.

No one has ever forced anyone to live without gas jets or to chuck the aspidistra in the bin – it's just that these things stopped making any sense

But there is a big difference with climate change. Within a generation everyone will have to live lighter. You will be the trendsetter, and everyone is going to follow you.

Chapter 3

You know it makes sense

Five great reasons for detoxing

As we found in Part 2, we all have different interests and motivations and will all find different reasons for living lighter. Here are five key ones written for a wide range of people. Winners will like reason one and will *love* reason five. Strivers will appreciate reason two. Reason four will chime with Traditionalists. There is a good reason here for anyone.

Reason 1: You get ahead of curve

The political consensus for action on climate change is developing rapidly. The only way that the government will have a hope in hell of meeting its emissions targets will be by aggressively taxing, banning, pillorying and squeezing high-emitting activities and correspondingly subsidizing, enabling, praising and generally massaging light living. When you detox you will be well positioned to benefit from these changes. People who hold back will be seriously penalized.

I'll bet there have been plenty of times when you have

been the first person you know to do something different: to use a new phrase, read a new book, have a certain style of clothes, buy a new gadget. You didn't see that as some radical 'alternative' statement – you saw it as smart and ahead of the curve. Before too long you noticed that everyone else was doing it – but they all know that you were the first to get there.

Throughout history there have always been people who embraced the future and chose to live differently, and there have always been people who resisted that change and were left behind

Take home lighting for example. Gas lighting first came into British homes in the mid-19th century, and I am sure that there were diehards who wanted to stick to their candles. And when the first electric lights came out people hated them. Students at Yale University took direct action and chopped down the first electric lamppost to appear on their campus. They said that they were 'getting more light than they relished'. Many people insisted on sticking with their gas jets, even though they suffocated everyone and left black streaks all over the ceiling.

And now I hear people say that they don't want to replace their incandescent light bulbs because they don't like the colour of the light from low-energy bulbs. This is a safe prediction: within a generation, incandescent light bulbs will exist only in a museum tableau of life in the 20th century. So do you want to live in a museum or the real world?

Reason 2: Your actions and your principles will dance together

It is a fundamental precept of human psychology that we seek a close balance between our principles and our actual behaviour. We can think of them as ballroom dancers – one leads and the other follows. Sometimes they pull apart and do a little twirl only to come together again with a flourish. When we are young they tango all over the dance floor, gyrating and throwing each other around. As we get older they move less and less, and I fear that they end up shuffling on the spot like the slow dance at the end of very drunken party.

We are uncomfortable when we notice a large gap opening up on the dance floor between our belief (that climate change is a major global problem) and our actions (the contribution that our own lifestyle is making to it). We have two options for bringing the dancers back together. We can change our lifestyle because we want our actions to follow our principles, or we can redefine our beliefs to suit our actions. Although we like to think that our internal principles lead our actions, more often than not it is our behaviour that sets the pace. The temptation, therefore, is to close the gap by persuading ourselves that maybe climate change is not such a big problem. As we saw in Part 4, there is a wide range of pick-and-mix excuses from which to choose when persuading ourselves that it is not happening, that the scientists haven't proved it, that someone else is causing it or that there is nothing that we can do about it.

When denial is so widespread and when there are so many temptations to ignore the problem light living is the only way in which we will be able to maintain our belief and be honest about the problem.

Reason 3: Smarter and happier

Look at the people in the checkout queue at any out-of-town shopping centre and ask: do they look as if the car and the motorway and all those rows of things to buy has made them any happier? What is so smart or satisfying about living this way?

Sociological research into personal happiness consistently finds that people are becoming unhappier, lonelier, more depressed and more stressed. By all these indicators, the highest level of personal happiness came in the mid-1970s and has been in steady decline ever since. The mid-1970s was also the take-off point for heavy-carbon living – the decade during which the luxuries of foreign flights and car ownership became not only normal but expected.

There are many reasons for this growth in unhappiness, and I would never claim that a heavy-carbon lifestyle is solely to blame, but surely we can say that the increases in affluence, energy consumption and mobility has done little to make us happier.

So, if you think it will be too difficult to halve our emissions just consider that we were already there one generation ago. And it was fine then. Now, I am not suggesting that we go back to the age of polyester flares and clackers. A lot of things have improved since then. Back in 1975 there was virtually no insulation or double glazing and gas central heating was considered modern. In winter my grandparents spent all day in the living room huddled round a coal fire while there was frost on the inside of their bedroom windows. I think I can do without that.

But it is interesting that, despite these huge increases in energy efficiency in the home, the introduction of new boilers and clean fuels have failed to stem the increase in our emissions. And, I ask again, are we actually any happier for it?

Reason 4: You are already halfway there

Do you leave your living room lights burning all night? I doubt it. Do you have hot water running constantly into the sink? Not unless you are nuts. Do you leave the car running overnight? Not unless you live in Siberia. Do you turn off the TV when you go to bed? I would imagine so (although I must confess that I once dealt with a period of insomnia by falling asleep to infomercials for fitness equipment).

If energy were free we would never turn anything off – but we are aware that it costs money and should not be wasted so we already practise a wide range of hands-on energy-conservation measures. Of course, they are not labelled as such in your mind – they are just things you do as part of your daily routine.

There may well be many other ways in which you are already 'living light' without even knowing it. My mother, for example, takes all of her holidays in the UK, buys locally produced food from local shops and turns off the heating in her bedroom. She doesn't do any of these things for the benefit of the climate – she does them because she likes them that way. Similarly, two-thirds of Londoners use the bus or Tube. I bet that no more than a handful of them do it as a conscious decision to be kind to the planet – for many of them, it simply makes more sense than travelling in London by car.

From the point of view of the climate it really doesn't matter why someone does something – it's what they burn that counts. So a large part of light living is absorbing these new patterns into your life so that you don't even think about them any more. Like my mother, you will do them because you like them that way.

Reason 5: You can buy some great stuff

If your great thrill in life is pulling something new out of a box – this applies especially to Winners – there is a bunch of light living kit that is fun and effective. See the Appendices for more details on how to get your hands on some of these gadgets (page 330).

Wireless electricity meter

To find out where your electricity is going you can buy a wireless meter (with a digital readout and lots of buttons) that you can put anywhere in the house or carry around with you. Friends who have them say that they get completely hooked going round the house switching things on and off and seeing where their power is going. The meters cost around £60.

Domestic renewable energy

Wind generators start at about £1,000, solar hot-water panels at around £3,000 and photovoltaic installations at about £5,000. All of these are big things that you can show to your neighbours and, like all fun electronic gadgets, they have controller boxes with digital read-outs and flashing diodes.

Vegetable fuel for cars

There are websites selling all you need to refit a diesel car so that it can run off vegetable oil. All over Britain there are small companies producing biodiesel that you can put directly into your car. There are some major issues with biodiesel, however. Large areas of Borneo's rainforest are being cleared to grow palm oil for biofuels, and world corn prices are rising because so much of the US corn production is being used this way. I recommend that you look for biofuel manufactured from waste cooking oil, which has no such problems and, smartest of all, your exhaust will smell ever so pleasantly of chips.

Induction hobs

I am dying to get one of these. Induction hobs cook by electromagnetic fields without any direct heat (please don't ask me how this works) and were first developed for use on ships. They are clean, cool in all senses of the word and use half the power of a normal hob.* And they are so clever that they can tell when something boils dry and switch off when you take away a pan. They are now already available from the major cooker manufacturers. You could be the first person on the street to own one.

Electric bicycles

This new generation of bicycles comes with a battery pack and small motor to help you up hills or give you that extra oomph. Surely a bicycle with extra power must be the perfect urban transport. They start at around £300.

LED lighting

The latest thing in lighting are bulbs made up from bundles of light-emitting diodes (LEDs). They use slightly less electricity than other low-energy bulbs and can replace halogen bulbs. And they will outlive your pet. They also put out a very nice, mellow light. Around £5 a bulb.

* It is important to point out that if you were using conventional electricity this would still entail higher emissions than a gas hob. However, an induction hob run on 'green' electricity is a really smart and low-carbon technology.

Wind-up radios and torches

I love these things – takes me back to the good old days of wind-up record players.

On the theme of fun things to buy, I cannot stress strongly enough that a detox lifestyle is about freeing yourself up to have fun. We are talking about living better by living differently. As we will see in the next chapter, that fun can include plenty of high-carbon treats, which, because they are rare and valued, become correspondingly memorable.

Chapter 4

Enjoy your treats
Why heavy-carbon fun still has a place in a light-carbon world

I want to stress that light living does not mean that you have to a wear horsehair shirt and beat yourself with nettles – although there are plenty of clubs for you to join if that is what you are into.

When it comes to climate change, the only important thing is the carbon bottom line (see pages 22–5). People who are living light will choose very different ways to live, and nowhere is this more evident than in the area of treats.

Treats are those occasional splurges that are fun, memorable and give you pleasure. Who would ever want to live in a world without them? Winners especially would feel utterly deprived if their treats were taken away. Treats may be extravagant, wasteful and decadent – that is what makes them treats, after all. As you will find when you do your life audit, it is the habitual 'heavy' behaviour that racks up the emissions, not the rare treat. Here are some ideas for treats that you can still have when you are living light, ranging from the budget to the extravagant.

• Spend all day in bed with someone you love.

• Elope and marry at Gretna Green.

• Smoke a Cuban cigar.

• Drive around the corner to buy a sandwich because it's raining and you don't want to get wet.

• Get drunk on champagne with your mates and sing your way home.

• Race a speedboat off the coast of Cornwall.

• Go for a full-throttle spin round a racetrack in a 6-litre sports car.

• Splurge on five courses and a bottle of superb wine at a fancy restaurant.

• Buy a season ticket for your favourite football team.

• Buy a pair of 'divine' Italian shoes.

• Spend a day watching the grand prix racing at Silverstone.

• Buy a stupidly expensive designer dress.

• Buy a new sound system with the woofiest speakers on earth.

• Whizz off to Paris by train for a romantic weekend at the Ritz.

- Get an au pair.

These are not, I am sure, the kinds of lifestyle options that usually appear in a book like this so I think they need explaining.

Climate unfriendly treats

Driving around the corner is not good for you or the world, but easy and handy once in a while. Green literature is scathing about unnecessary local car trips. They create congestion and urban pollution and make roads unsafe for children. I agree, and later in this book I recommend that you ditch the car. But in terms of the carbon bottom line it is habitual, long-distance driving that is the problem, so let's get our priorities right.

And how about those speed treats? Of course, sports cars and speedboats drink fuel, but there is no reason why we could not experience the adrenaline of speed as a special treat. At the risk of being a rambling bore, I say again that it is the habitual, steady burning of petrol that is an issue, not the once-in-a-while splurge. Even if I ran a Ferrari Testarossa round a racetrack at full whack for 20 minutes I would still only have burned as much petrol as I would driving our sluggish Volvo estate to visit my mum. Come on kids, which one would you rather do?

Luxury products

Luxury clothes and shoes have no more climate impact than cheap ones. The difference in price is due to labour, advertising and profit, not energy. The issue is much more a matter of how much you buy rather than what you buy, and if something fancy gives you a thrill, then fine.

Some products do have significant climate impacts. Electrical goods, for example, have considerable embodied emissions from the energy and solvents involved in their manufacture, and they consume electricity to run. However, this does not mean that you can't buy an excellent quality audio system that you will love and will give you real pleasure. In any case, the resources that go into a quality product may well be the same as go into a crummy one that breaks within a year.

Special events

Fancy meals are occasional things that register in our memories. Given that the best chefs use local organic ingredients in tiny portions, a meal in a fancy restaurant will probably produce lower emissions than the mixed grill in your local café.

Special overseas trips are fine once in a while providing they don't involve flying. Mass events – football matches, plays, films, even car racing – produce lower emissions than the audience would if it stayed at home. The real climate impact of any mass event lies in the transport that gets the audience there. And, even better, parties, boozy nights out and all varieties of rumpy-pumpy are effectively carbon neutral.

People are carbon neutral

Finally, a word for rich people. I fear I can't persuade you to give your money away, so if you want to live light but are wondering what on earth you can spend your money on if you can't have your flash car or fly out every other weekend to your holiday home in Tuscany. I have just two words – buy people.

175

You can buy as many people as you can afford. You can hire an artist to paint murals of your entire lineage up and down the stairs. You can pay a team of gardeners to plant your own arboretum. You can have maids, au pairs, butlers and cooks so that you never have to lift a finger. And if your 'helpers' live with you, your home becomes 'a house of multiple occupancy', and that's even better.

And on that note, fearing that every anti-globalization class-war anarchist in east Oxford will hunt me down and stone me to death, I suggest we move quickly on.

Chapter 5

Find a lifestyle that says nice things about you

How our choices are made by the stories we tell ourselves

The publishing sensation of the 2000s was a glossy and irritating design magazine called *Wallpaper*. I read it because I am genuinely interested in modern design, but I hardly think that I am the target audience for a £140,000 Lamborghini Murciélago or a £25,000 Hastens Vividus bed. They are looking for rich mugs, not tatty writers in second-hand shirts.

The adverts in *Wallpaper* tell us a great deal about personal motivation. The images and language appeal strongly to individuality and conviction. They are aimed at the very richest of the Winners described on pages 46–50. 'Courage to express who you are' sells a three-piece suite. 'Drink life deeply' advertises the appropriately named Knob Whiskey. Hitachi Hi-Fi comes with the slogan 'Inspire the next'.

Inspire the next *what*? Next credit card bill? Next complaint from your neighbour about the noise?

And how about this paean to higher values: 'What is it that sets some people apart? It's the way they act. And interact only with that which is true to their values. Like integrity and provenance.' And clean armpits – this ad is selling showers.

What is interesting about these advertisements is that they say next to nothing about the product. The advert is designed to provide cues for how they will make the purchasers feel about themselves.

What your things say about you

The things we buy and the way we live are seldom conscious or rational choices. As advertisers know, we buy the things we do because they tell a story about us. They say: I am successful. I am rich. I am modern. I am attractive. I am popular. I am a good mother. I am a sexy beast of a man. We also buy things to say what we are not. Again marketers and advertisers are wise to this – for example, by advertising street fashion with the message 'your dad wouldn't like it'.

The main reasons people continue to buy into the heavy-carbon lifestyle are because they are told that it shows them in a positive and flattering light. Owning a car and having regular foreign holidays are, for many people, a badge of their personal attainment, regardless of whether they really need or enjoy these things.

What detoxing will say about you

• I am no longer weighed down by all those old 20th-century ideas about what is smart or cool or free. Everything is changing and I am in tune with the times because I am a light-living person who embraces the challenges of the 21st century.

• I am light, trim, efficient, effective, ahead of the curve and in the moment. I am no longer heavy, weighed down by carbon and things that I don't need or locked in to decisions made by someone else about what I should be or have.

• I am going to reject all of those commercial messages that tell me that I am not attractive, clever or successful because I choose to live differently. I know that this is a lie to play on my insecurities.

• I am never going to listen when someone tells me that a car or holiday will make me 'free'. I will choose my own freedom. Marketers say that people are 'locked in' to brands and lifestyles. I can't see anything very free about being 'locked' into anything.

And when you are about to do something or buy something, stop, think and ask yourself: 'That thing I am about to do or buy – does it say that I am the person I used to be or the person I want to be?'

Chapter 6

Unfreeze your habits
Why habits are useful and how you can create new ones

We make so many decisions every day about what to buy and do that we would go mad if we had to weigh up every single decision independently and rationally. So that we can function and get through the day, we depend on a set of mental short-cuts that draw on our past behaviour and expectations to make decisions for us. Social psychologists call these short-cuts 'heuristics'. I will call them habits, but bear in mind that the meaning is more complex than this word normally suggests.

The vast bulk of our decisions are so guided by habit that we don't even think about them: we never consciously decide which side to get out of bed, which key opens the front door, which brand of teabags to buy or where to stand in a crowd. Habit decides for us.

You soon discover the power of habit when you try shopping for familiar ingredients in a new country. Decisions that are usually made in a daze by reaching for the familiar brands and recognizable packaging become painfully hard. I remember being transfixed and paralysed in an American supermarket by 28 different brands of mustard – yes I really did count them – that all looked exactly the same. A woman took pity on me and said, 'Try this one. It's what I always buy.' And that brand then became the one that I always bought. Branding, you see, is all about setting consumer habits.

Habit also guides decisions that we think long and hard about. We go back to the same place for a holiday. We buy a house like the one we had last time. Or, on a more subtle level, we buy the house like the one we grew up in or that we understand is appropriate for someone of our class and style. In the last chapter we found that our behaviour is often led by the stories we tell ourselves, and these stories, too, can become so deeply engrained in our thinking that they become habits.

Here is a good example. Many of the people in my part of Oxford are middle-class Strivers. They are concerned about climate change and try in various ways to live lighter. And yet I will bet that every one of them is prepared to pay a premium for the privilege of living in a hopelessly inefficient, cold and draughty Victorian house rather than a modern house that burns half as much fuel.

They claim that they want to live in their old house because it looks nicer or because they just happen to 'like old things', but I am not persuaded. After all, they don't drive vintage cars or wear vintage clothes, even though they are old and also look nicer. I think that their choices are actually being led by a set of habits drawn from their class, childhood and the stories they tell themselves about who they are: 'People like me live like this'. As I said in Part 2, in spite of their concerns, Strivers are perfectly capable to ratcheting up high emissions.

Detoxing means challenging and changing your habits

You will need to recognize that habitual behaviour is often reinforced by short-term benefits – convenience, familiarity and speed. As you develop your various strategies you will find opportunities to strategically 'unfreeze' familiar patterns. Once you have reconsidered them you can then freeze them back into new 'light' habits.

Big purchasing decisions are always conscious but often guided by the story you want to tell about yourself. For these you will need to ask: is this decision being guided by my old habits or the new story I want to tell about myself?

The majority of our day-to-day emissions come from behaviour that is unconscious and rarely challenged. Do you ever really consider how long you spend in the shower, how much water you put in the kettle, how you drive or which vegetables you buy? Or do you just do what you did last time and the time before?

Throughout the detox process you will be invited to change your habits. You will be asked to choose a day or a week during which you actively unfreeze your habits and challenge them. You will create new habits and, once they are guiding your decisions, you will automatically live lighter.

Part 8
Counting the carbos

Chapter 1

Counting counts

Why only counting can find those carbon-heavy areas

So far I have carefully avoided all references to diets. Diets are all about giving things up. Living light is really much more like healthy eating than a diet. Nonetheless, there is one very useful thing we can learn from dieting: counting calories.

Though calorie counting dieters can find out exactly where their calories are coming from so that they can develop a really effective strategy for cutting back. They tend to find that there are a few big-calorie items – such as booze, chocolates, pizzas or chips – that account for a large part of the problem and can be easily dealt with.

Despite this, dieters can get things completely wrong. Ever since the 1920s fashionable diets have demanded a daily dose of grapefruit as though this wretched sour fruit has some magic power to neutralize fats. In fact, it has the same number of calories as an orange. Or take salads. Without calorie counting one can pretend that a salad is slimming, even when those green lettuce leaves are just providing camouflage for fatty items such as thick mayonnaise, potato salads or scotch eggs (which, let's face it, are just a deep-fried sausage in breadcrumbs).

It is just the same with climate change. If we don't know the emissions of our different activities, we are likely to pretend that the things we like are OK or instead fixate on things that make very little difference (See Plastic bag fetish, pages 126–8). So we need to calculate our real impacts.

Now I am no fan of forms. The bailiffs were beating a track up my path to remove the TV by the time I could summon up the energy to fill in my last tax return. However this is important. As I have said all along, the only thing that actually counts is the carbon bottom line. If you are serious about your carbon detox you really *have* to do some maths to find out where your emissions are coming from.

Introducing the carbo

You are going to measure your real impacts using a new unit called the 'carbo'.

This is why we need a new unit: most of your emissions will be in carbon dioxide, but, as we shall see you will also be responsible for some far more powerful greenhouse gases, such as methane and nitrous oxides. I have combined these different climate impacts into one unit, the carbo, which has the same climate-change effect as 1 kg (2.2 lb) of carbon dioxide. A kilo of methane, which has 23 times the climate impact of a kilo of carbon dioxide, is 23 carbos. As you will see, bringing everything together in one measure will make your calculations far easier and make everything directly comparable. In technical papers a carbo would be called 'one kilogram of carbon dioxide equivalent', which is sometimes abbreviated to CO_2e.

What you will be doing

Over the next five chapters you will find out your exact personal contribution to climate change and where it is coming from. You will break down everything you do into five categories – house, land transport, aeroplanes and boats, food, and goods and services – and then you will calculate your carbos for each one. Once you have all these figures you will add all the services you receive through the government because, even though you don't get any real choice over them, the government's choices contribute to your total impacts.

How you will be doing it

For most categories you have a choice between a quick-and-easy calculation and a more fancy, detailed one. The quick-and-easy version will give you a ballpark figure so that you can get a rough idea of your emissions. But it will only be rough because it is based on national averages and makes no allowance for how you actually live. By this reckoning my carbon twin neighbour, who lives in exactly the same house as me, would get the same score even though I am sure he is eating up energy. So I strongly recommend that you try to do the more complex version if you can.

There is no great maths in this – all you need is a calculator. Once you have the figure I ask for you simply multiply it by the figure in the circle and write the sum in the box

This process will take a few minutes but it will be interesting, I promise. I have led many workshops through it, and I have never had a group that wasn't completely amazed by the results.

You will find out many things that are unexpected including:

- Why a leaky uninsulated student house can do better than a highly insulated house next door.

- How travelling by car can be better for the climate than travelling by train.

- How a single flight can do more damage than heating your house for a decade.

- How a short commute to work does more harm than driving to Bahrain.

- And why a liner can be the worst travel option of all.

Chapter 2
Where you live
Home energy

We are going to start with your home, for most people the single largest source of their emissions. I have two different counters here – a quick-and-easy version and a fancy version. The results from the quick version are not very accurate and make no allowance for how you actually live, so do the fancy version if at all possible.

The quick-and-easy version

Only do this easy carbo-counter if you are in a hurry. Otherwise go on to the fancy version on pages 192–3.

Section 1

Heating	Carbos
Do you heat with wood	Go to section 2
Start with the kind of house you live in	
A flat	2,100
A terrace or semi-detached	4,300
A large house	5,800

Do you heat with

Gas	Keep your total
Electricity	Double your total
Oil or coal	Increase your total by half again

Now energy efficiency

Do you have a condensing boiler?	Take a quarter off your total
Do you have solar hot water?	Take off 500

Heating subtotal

Section 2

Electricity   **Carbos**

Do you use

'Green' electricity?	Enter zero in the electricity subtotal

Do you live in

A flat	Add 800
A terrace or semi-detached	Add 1,600
A large house	Add 2,500

Electricity subtotal

Now add together the heating and electricity totals and divide by the number of people who live in the house.

**Total house emissions
per person per year**

Enter this figure in row 1 on the table on page 227

The fancy version

Before you fill in this version, you need the answers to a few questions.

Where do I find the figures for the house?

The best sources are the meter readings on your old bills. Try to avoid the estimated readings if you can. Energy consumption changes throughout the year, so you need to find readings from the same quarter in different years. The results will be even more accurate if you can find readings that are several years apart.

If you don't have fuel bills to hand you can call up the power company, which will provide the old figures over the phone, even if you have since switched to another supplier. If you are in a hurry and just want to get on with it and you know approximately how much you spend in fuel bills, then go ahead and use the rough calculation based on your costs, but the results will be much less accurate.

I have a holiday home. Do I count that too?

You count emissions for every house you live in. If you share or rent out a holiday home, then only include the proportion of energy from your personal use.

I work from home. Do I include this?

No. We are only looking at your personal lifestyle not your work. If you use your home for work purposes deduct the percentage or the house area that is for work use.

I live with other people. How do I work out my share?

You need to start with the total figure for the house, then divide it by the number of people who use it.

Do kids count as people?

At the end of a long day you may seriously wonder. For the purposes of the carbo-counter, I suggest that you count children over the age of four as a whole person. Although babies and toddlers take up space and require lots of washing, they are economical in other ways, so I suggest counting them as a half.

I have photovoltaic panels or a wind generator and sell my electricity back to the grid. What happens here?

More and more people are fitting home solar panels on their roofs and selling their surplus electricity back to the grid. Because this is replacing conventional electricity, I think it is fair to multiply the electricity you sell by 0.43 and deduct this from your overall total.

Enough questions – this isn't a tax form! If in doubt, use your common sense

Home power

Find the best figures you can *for a whole year*. Then
multiply by the carbo multiplier to find your carbos.

	Your figure	Multiplier	Your carbos
Gas heating			
New-style units (cubic metres) of mains gas		x 2.2	
Or old-style units (100s cubic feet) of mains gas		x 6.2	
Or kilowatt hours (kWh) equivalent		x 0.2	
Or, if you can't find any other figures: What is the cost (in £) of your annual gas bills?		x 5	
Heating oil			
Litres of heating oil		x 3	
Gallons of heating oil		x 13.6	
Coal			
Kilograms of anthracite coal		x 2.5	
Kilograms of bituminous coal		x 1.9	
(Note: one sack of coal usually weighs 50 kg/110 lb)			
LPG			
Kilowatt hours		x 0.2	
Wood, hydro		x 0	

Conventional electricity
Kilowatt hours
(kWh) ⬜ x 0.43 ⬜

Or, if you can't find any other figures:
What is the cost (in £) of
your annual electricity bills? ⬜ x 5.3 ⬜

'Green' electricity
This is electricity that is
guaranteed to come from
renewable sources
Kilowatt hours (kWh) ⬜ x 0 ⬜

Subtotal ⬜

Now, if you work from home, deduct a
percentage for the area of your house given
over to work ⬜

Total home power ⬜

Now divide by the number of people who
share the house ⬜

Total house impact per person ⬜

Enter this figure in row 1 on the table on page 227

Carbo lessons

1 The biggest determinant of house emissions is the level of occupancy

Yes, it's true. Imagine that you are living on your own. If you do all the right things – insulate your loft and all your cavity walls, fit a condensing boiler, double-glaze your windows – you may be able to halve your emissions. You would have the same effect if you did nothing except take in a lodger. This is why the most efficient houses are those that are fully occupied by a family or with multiple occupancy. A run-down, leaky, old property let out to students will very likely have better emissions per person than the other houses on the street, even though their windows are open all day so they can blast reggae across the neighbourhood.

It is a mystery to me why government strategies for reducing emissions from housing never seek to increase house-occupancy levels or encourage people to downsize to smaller properties. It seems crazy that that there are many older people living on their own in a large family house because they can't face the trauma of moving. Surely they could be given help to move to a more suitable property?

2 Electricity is very high in carbos

Conventional electricity is extremely inefficient. Scarcely a third of the heat produced by burning coal or gas is turned into electricity. The rest is thrown away in the cooling towers. Then there are further losses in the transformers and power lines before it reaches our houses. In clever countries, such as Sweden and the Netherlands, they use the waste heat in houses or greenhouses. In Britain we are so disorganized that we chuck it away.

For these reasons it seems daft to use electricity for

heating. In my view storage heaters should be banned. However, electricity does have one big advantage over other fuels – flexibility. You can plug in a fan heater or bar fire exactly where you want it. Even though electricity seems wasteful it does make sense to use an electric heater if you want a little heat in just one room – for example, if you are working from home.

3 'Green' electricity saves a lot of carbos

Yes, there is a huge saving. And switching to renewable power sends a powerful message through the energy market. Although green electricity is listed on this table as having no carbos, it is not entirely carbon free – there *are* emissions involved with building windmills and dams, generating the power and transmitting it through the grid. But these emissions are very small compared with the electricity generated. For the same reason, the calculator for conventional electricity doesn't include emissions from building power plants or shipping coal around the world.

As you can see, some themes are already emerging. We can see that there are huge differences between different fuels and heating technologies. And we find that no matter how efficient our home, occupancy levels are crucial. These conclusions are further strengthened in the next section – personal transport.

Chapter 3

How you get about
Land transport

Personal transport already accounts for 12 per cent of an average person's emissions and is rising rapidly. Once again I have two different counters here – a quick-and-easy version for an approximate figure and a fancy version for an accurate figure.

The quick-and-easy version

Only use this easy carbocounter if you are in a hurry. Otherwise go on to the fancy version on pages 200–201.

Section 1

Car	Carbos
I do not drive	Go to section 2
Do you own you own car?	Start with 300
Do you drive under 8,000 km (5,000 miles) a year for personal use?	Add 1,100
For each additional 8,000 km (5,000 miles) for personal use	Add 1,100

Has your car got an engine larger
than 2 litres?   Add a quarter

Does your car have a diesel engine?   Deduct a third

Driving subtotal

**Now divide by the number of
people who use the car**

Total car emissions per person

Enter this figure in row 2 of the table on page 227

Section 2

Public transport	Carbos
I never use public transport	Skip this section

For every hour you spend in an average week

On a commuter train	Add 300
On an intercity train	Add 450
On a city bus	Add 150
On an inter-city bus	Add 200
On the underground	Add 160

Total public transport emissions

Enter this figure in row 3 of the table on page 227

The fancy version

You need the answers to a few questions before you can fill in this form.

Where do I find the figures for a car?

The most accurate carbo result would be from the litres of petrol that your car uses in the course of a year. Alternatively, if you keep receipts for your petrol you could divide them by the current cost of petrol per litre. Another alternative is to multiply your annual mileage by the fuel consumption declared by the manufacturer in the car manual. Since 2001 manufacturers have also had to declare the emissions of the car as grams of carbon dioxide per kilometre. Multiply this figure by kilometres travelled and multiply by 1,000 to find your carbos.

The problem with using these estimates is that they are obtained under optimal test conditions, and it is clearly in the interests of the manufacturer to get the best result possible. Actual performance can be up to a third worse. If you are interested in finding your real performance you could start to keep a diary in the glove compartment to record your mileage against fuel consumption and see how it compares.

Do I include my travel for work?

No. We are only looking at your personal lifestyle, not your work. If you use your home or car for work deduct the percentage of mileage that is for work use.

Do I include my travel to work?

Yes. This counts as personal emissions. After all, you do have some control over where you live and how you travel to work.

I share my car with other people – how do I work out my emission?

You need to start with the total figures for the car. Then divide by the number of people who use it. Don't be sneaky and assume that everyone has the same share of a car. I will bet that, sometimes, it is used just for your own purposes. So reckon on a reasonable balance – if you have a family of four but you use it exclusively half the time, then you can reckon on an average use by two people.

Section 1: Car use

Find the best figures you can *for a whole year*. Then multiply by the carbo multiplier to find your carbos.

The most accurate way to calculate emissions is using fuel consumption and then multiplying by the figures below.

Fuel		Carbo multiplier	Carbos
Litres petrol		x 2.3	
Gallons petrol		x 10.4	
Litres diesel		x 2.7	
Gallons diesel		x 12.2	

Or, to get your annual fuel consumption, divide your total annual distance by the manufacturer's stated fuel consumption. Then multiply by gallons or litres as above.

Or, if all this fails, use the rough (and not very accurate) rule of thumb below for petrol engines. Diesel engines will produce on average a third less carbon per mile.

Different car types
Small car: 1.4 litre engine

Miles		x 0.28	
Kilometres		x 0.17	

Medium car: 1.4 to 2.1 litre engine

Miles		x 0.36	
Kilometres		x 0.22	

Large car: Over 2.1litre engine

Miles		x 0.43	
Kilometres		x 0.27	

Your total fuel carbos

If you own a car add 300 for the emissions that went into making it

Your total car emissions

Deduct a percentage or mileage for any use of your car for work

Total household car use

Now divide this by the number of people who use the car

Total car emissions per person

Section 2: Public transport

For public transport you will need to find some distances.

Distance travelled	Carbo multiplier	Carbos
Rail		
Kilometres	x 0.06	
Miles	x 0.12	
Underground/commuter electric rail/tram		
Kilometres	x 0.1	
Miles	x 0.17	
Urban bus		
Kilometres	x 0.1	
Miles	x 0.17	
Long-distance bus		
Kilometres	x 0.05	
Miles	x 0.08	
Total public emissions transport		

Enter these figures in rows 2 and 3 of the table on page 227

Carbo lessons

1 Once again everything depends on how many people use a car

Here's an interesting question: how can you double the fuel efficiency of your car? No fancy technology is needed: just put someone in the passenger seat.

We know that public transport is more efficient because lots of people use the same vehicle, but we don't recognize that exactly the same can be said about houses and cars. If just half of the people driving to work on their own could be persuaded to double up with another driver we could eliminate most traffic jams without a single inch more tarmac.

2 Public transport is better than cars, but not *that* much better

During rush hour trains and buses are packed to the gills and have far, far lower emissions than cars with only one person in them. However, while cars are used only when needed, trains and buses have to run throughout the day to maintain a full service. Much of this time they are seriously underused. Once this is taken into consideration, the relative advantage of public transport is greatly eroded. It is clear from the carbo-counter (based on Railtrack's own carbon audit) that a car with four people in it will have lower emissions per passenger than a train.

Now please don't misunderstand me. There are many, many problems with cars other than simply their fuel use. They pollute the air, disrupt and break up communities and kill thousands of people a year. I am not arguing that cars are better than public transport, nor am I writing off public transport. Buses and trains have a vital role in a light-carbon economy, and if they got the government support that they deserve they would be far better filled.

What I *am* saying though is that, once again, the only thing that counts for climate change is the carbon bottom line. Taking public transport is still better than a car, but it is all a matter of degree and there can still be a place for a well-filled car in a light lifestyle.

3 Commuting clocks up a staggering number of miles

The average British worker commutes nearly 4,800 kilometres (3,000 miles) a year. If you commute by public transport you will already have been surprised by how rapidly a daily commute of a few kilometres clocks up. In fact, if you want to be precise, within a year, a daily train commute to work of 20 kilometres (12½ miles) each way will reach the same total distance as the 9,000 kilometre (5,600 mile) Trans-Siberian Railway, even allowing for a long holiday to recover.

Or, if you commute by car, you can think of it this way. Every 3 months of driving 10 kilometres (6 miles) to work and back is the equivalent of driving to the south of France. Wouldn't you rather be doing that? This is yet further proof that we do not have to give up treats and thrills in order to live lightly. We can still have an even better life if we can rethink where our emissions are coming from.

4 Your car still has a major climate impact even if it never leaves the drive

Cars are the single most energy-intensive product we own – just think of the energy that went into making all that steel and plastic. The manufacture of an average car produces 5 tonnes of carbon dioxide, of which only 1 tonne is recovered when the car is scrapped. That leaves 4 tonnes of emissions for every car. It is only reasonable that these emissions are shared equally between all the people who own it, after all the only reason second-hand cars exist is because someone once bought them with a view to selling them later.

Given that the average UK car lasts for 13 years, car owners are responsible for 300 carbos per year for the emissions that went into making it. Sorry to tell you, even if your car is 20 years old, it is still not carbon neutral: it is just making up for the car that conked out before it reached its thirteenth birthday.

Now, bearing in mind what you have clocked up so far, let's take a look at what flying does to your overall figures. Before you turn the page, though, a quick question. How many years do you think you would need to heat your house before you ran up as much of an impact on the climate as a return flight to Australia?

Chapter 4

How you travel abroad
Aeroplanes and boats

International travel is the elephant in the room, the thing that no one wants to challenge or talk about. We think we love it, we think we have earned the right to do it, and we will fight tooth and nail with anyone who tries to take it away. As we shall see, though, it is a very heavy-carbon item that can easily outweigh all your other emissions put together.

A few quick questions

Before filling in the form, you will need the answers to the following questions.

I offset my flights to make them 'carbon neutral'. Do I still count them?

Many people who are concerned about their flights pay a surcharge to a company that offers to 'offset' their emissions by funding an activity elsewhere that will save the same amount of emissions.

Personally, however, I think they should be included in your personal account because you still make the emissions and they are still on your bottom line. It is an excellent idea to give money to people who are planting trees or giving solar panels to Indian villages, and we count this later as 'zero-carbon' spending, but I don't think this in any way changes the fact that the greenhouses gases from your flight are now in the air and causing trouble.

I have to add that offset companies often indulge in some very creative accounting to support their figures. As we discover below, they routinely underestimate flight emissions by two-thirds and they tend to exaggerate the amount of carbon that their projects save. So my personal view is that your flight emissions still count. If you disagree with me and believe that you have effectively neutralized the climate impact of your flights don't count them.

I fly a lot for my work. Do I count these flights?

No. We are measuring your personal emissions. Of course, you should still be doing what you can to minimize work flights as part of your commitment to engage with climate change.

I used an online carbon calculator to work out my flights and I got a much lower figure. Why is this?

Ah, that's probably because the calculator was run by a company that wanted to sell you offsets and it fixed the figures so that it didn't look as if it would cost too much to make the flight 'carbon neutral'. As we shall see, government and industrial bodies routinely understate the real climate impacts of flying.

Planes

For a good approximation when calculating emissions take the following figures for return flights.

Destination	Carbos
Short haul (within UK, Paris, Amsterdam)	500
Eastern Europe	800
East Africa	3,200
Middle East	3,200
East coast USA	4,000
India	5,000
West coast USA	5,800
East Asia	6,400
South Africa	6,500
Japan	6,500
Australia	11,000
New Zealand	12,200

Or you can get an approximate number on the distance covered.

	Kilometres travelled	Carbo multiplier	Carbos
Short-haul flights		x 0.5	
Long-haul flights		x 0.3	

Boats

For slow ferries multiply the kilometres travelled by 0.1

For fast ferries multiply by 0.5

For liners and cruise ships multiply by 0.7 or multiply the days at sea by 230.

Total emissions from air and sea travel

Enter this figure in row 4 of the table on page 227

Carbo lessons

1 Flying has a much greater impact that you would think

As you can see, you don't have to fly very far before a single flight has made a greater climate impact than a whole year of heating your house. If you are a family of four living in an average suburban semi, then a holiday in Australia will have the same climate impact as heating your house for a decade or leaving your TV on standby for 234 years.

If you have the habit, and the money to feed it, you can run up huge climate impacts through flying. The high speed and relatively low cost encourages us to make regular journeys that might otherwise might be too daunting by other means. The ship journey to Australia used to take six weeks and was so long and tedious that it would take people who emigrated years before they could face the journey back to visit the old country. Now many emigrants fly to and fro every year or more often.

This much is obvious. The second reason for the high impact of flying is less well known: burning fuel in jet engines at high altitude has nearly *three times the climate impact* of burning the same amount of fuel in a car at ground level. The carbon dioxide is the least of it. The very high temperatures inside jet engines also create nitrous oxides, which are very powerful greenhouse gases, 310 times more powerful than carbon dioxide.

And jet planes also produce vapour trails called contrails. If you live under a flight path you will notice on a still day that the entire sky is crossed with vapour trails that steadily spread out to cover much of the sky and form high-level cirrus clouds. These, too, are heat trapping, especially at night.

There are still no firm conclusions about the total impact on climate change of jet planes, and many factors are yet to be fully explored. On the basis of the current science the IPCC has concluded that the total climate change impacts of jet planes are 2.8 times greater than the impact of the carbon dioxide alone.

So isn't it interesting that airline representatives conveniently ignore all these other factors when they answer media enquiries about the impacts of aviation? They argue that aviation produces 'just' 5 per cent of UK CO_2 emissions'. It is a classic distortion to focus on just one aspect of something damaging. It is rather like tobacco companies talking only about the health impacts of the nicotine in a cigarette.

You will also notice that government spokespeople use the same false statistics. Although they like to talk up strong action on climate change, they have no desire to take on the powerful aviation lobby or to risk a tabloid meltdown by seriously curtailing air travel. A recent report by the Tyndall Centre for Climate Change Research pointed out that the real climate impact of the planned predicted doubling in air traffic over the next 30 years will swamp all other government targets to deal with climate change.

2 Boats are sometimes no better than planes – at the moment

Ships are glorious things, and I love travelling on them. But they are not necessarily an efficient form of transport. Like trains, we see them through a romantic glow of the 'golden age of travel' – golden, that is, for the people who didn't have to spend the whole trip on a bunk in the bilges.

Ships are certainly efficient for cargo – they are huge and slow and carry up to 14,000 containers at a time. They are also efficient when they are slow and plodding like old-style ferries, with emissions that are similar to those of trains. But, because of the resistance of water, fuel consumption increases dramatically with speed. A fast ferry will use four times as much fuel as a slow one. And on long-distance journeys people want both speed and space. Every passenger, whatever their class, requires somewhere to sleep, somewhere to eat, somewhere to wash, somewhere to get fresh air and a large crew to provide for them. And the crew needs these things too. All of this adds to the size and weight of a passenger boat.

A plane is made from high-performance aluminium and weighs only 0.2 tonnes per passenger. A modern liner has to carry 40 tonnes of steel for every passenger. So, even though boats are far more efficient than planes for moving cargo, they would need to be 200 times more efficient to even equal a plane for carrying passengers.

And they are not. The full climate impacts of a return flight across the Atlantic is the equivalent of $4\frac{1}{2}$ tonnes of carbon dioxide. The impacts of the same journey in a fast-moving liner like the *QE2* is over 9 tonnes. Now the *QE2* is a luxury liner, it is true, but it is still hard to imagine that the she could beat a jumbo unless it took twice as long and everyone was sleeping in dormitories and living on sandwiches . . . unless it was converted to a troop ship in other words.

Now, this is not to write off any role for ships in a light-carbon future. There are immense opportunities for improving the performance of marine engines. Recent experiments have augmented the engines with sails. At the same time, jet planes are reaching the limits of their technology. They will get a bit lighter, a bit bigger, use a bit less fuel and be better managed around airports, but it is unlikely that there will be any further leaps in efficiency. My money is on ships in the longer term, even if they are not looking like a great option right now.

Chapter 5

What you eat
Food

Of all the goods and services you buy, it is food that has the greatest climate change impact. It is also the area in which your personal choices produce the greatest variations. If you lived solely on fruit and vegetables grown on your own allotment, you would have no emissions at all – in fact, your veggie plot could well be soaking up carbon from the air.

These figures in this carbo-counter account for the energy used in agriculture, fertilizers, food transport, processing, storage, shops and catering. They also include the methane and nitrous oxide from animals, animal wastes and agricultural soil.

Food

In the categories marked * you may wish to adjust the figures up or down according to your personal usage.

Food	Carbos
A typical British diet with 38 per cent of nutrition animal based	Start with 2,000*
A serious meat diet (50 per cent animal based)	Start with 2,250*

A light meat diet (a little meat once a day or less)	Start with 1,750*
A vegetarian diet (replacing the meat in a typical diet with dairy)	Start with 1,500
A vegan diet (no animal products at all)	Start with 1,000
If you eat only organically produced food	Halve your score (or the relevant proportion)
If you eat meat that is not organic but *is* free range	Deduct 100
If you never eat beef or lamb	Deduct 200
If **nearly all** your food is processed and/or imported	Add 200
If you buy air-freight fish or vegetables once a month	Add another 40
If **very little** of your food is processed and/or imported	Deduct 400
If you eat all leftovers and never throw away edible food	Deduct 10 per cent
If you compost all of your food waste	Deduct 200

Eating out

About 25 per cent of meals in the UK are eaten away from home.

If you **hardly ever** eat in restaurants or canteens	Deduct 100
If you eat **half your meals** in restaurants or canteens	Add 100
If half your meals are takeaways that you take home	Add 50

Your total food impacts

Enter this figure in row 5 of the table on page 227

Carbo lessons

1 Conventional agriculture is far worse than organic agriculture

What is the single largest cause of emissions in the food you eat? Agricultural machinery, road transport, air freight, supermarkets, cows burping? All wrong, I'm afraid. By far the largest cause, responsible for 450 carbos in the average diet, are the nitrous oxides produced when nitrogen-based fertilizers break down in the soil. As we found in the last chapter, nitrous oxide is a very powerful greenhouse gas and has 310 times the global-warming power of carbon dioxide.

This means that avoiding the use of artificial fertilizers is a hugely important issue for preventing climate change

But organic agriculture is important for other reasons too. The use of natural fertilizers from vegetable and animal manure returns their carbon to the soil. In industrialized agriculture animal manure is often treated as a waste and is thrown away or stored in large open ponds that generate methane. And finally, because it takes many kilos of crops to produce a kilo of meat, these differences become even more pronounced in organic meat. Organic meat is usually free range, too, which leads to yet lower climate impacts.

I must stress, though, that this is a complex area. The animal manure and nitrogen-fixing fallow crops used as fertilizers in organic agriculture will also release some nitrous oxides. Land under organic management often requires more ploughing for weed removal, and this can leads to higher carbon dioxide emissions. Nonetheless, the overall balance of emissions is still strongly in favour of organic production.

Although many people find it hard to afford organic produce, I suspect that many others don't feel that it is something for them, because it is marketed as a trendy lifestyle statement for fit, good-looking people who play too much squash. Well, not so – even I buy it and no one would recognize me from that description. This is another case where we need to ignore the messenger and look at the carbon bottom line. Taken together, the overall emissions for food from organic farming are half of those for food from conventional farming. So the single most effective way that you can reduce food emissions is by going organic.

2 A vegetable diet can be worse for the climate than a meat diet

I don't want to underplay the impacts of meat eating. The average Briton munches through nearly 100 kg (220 lb) of meat a year, and that's a pretty disgusting thought. Meat production uses a lot of land, water and energy, and many factory-farmed animals have short, miserable and painful lives. And it is clear from the carbo-counter that a heavy meat diet will have major climate impacts. For all these reasons some people are rightly worked up about meat.

However, it is not true, as vegetarian enthusiasts claim, that giving up meat is the single most important thing that you can do for climate change. A vegetarian diet can easily clock up more emissions than a moderate meat one. For example, many vegetarians I know seem to live on out-of-season Mediterranean vegetables fried up with a tin of tomatoes and served with rice. This diet will produce more emissions than a meat-based diet that uses local organic produce. Check the carbo-counter if you don't believe me.

And the difference is even greater for vegetarians eating a lot of dairy products and processed foods.

Aha – strike one for eco-mincetarians!

3 Not all meat is equal

There are enormous differences between the various kinds of meat. Kilo for kilo, lamb and beef have four times the carbos of pork and eight times the carbos of chicken. Even organic, free-range beef is four times worse than a factory-farmed chicken. The difference is all down to the prodigious quantities of methane burped up by cows and sheep as a by-product of their digestion of the cellulose in grass, a process known technically as 'enteric fermentation'.

In a year, a cow will produce 120 kg (265 lb) of methane, which, as a powerful greenhouse gas, is the equivalent of 2.8 tonnes of carbon dioxide. That is the equivalent of driving a car for 10,000 kilometres (6,200 miles). Imagine that every cow in Britain was commuting 28 kilometres (17 miles) to her field and back each day and you have an idea of the problem. Of course, it would be loads better if they shared their bloody cars, but they just refuse to budge up.

In terms of their size, sheep are even worse burpers than cows, which is why they are the single largest source of greenhouse gases in New Zealand

4 Wasting food piles on the carbos

Individuals vary widely in terms of their attitudes to leftovers and food waste. Some people compost all waste and keep creatively reinventing leftovers in new guises until they all get used up. And some people throw all uneaten food straight in the bin without a second's thought.

There are very considerable differences between the climate-change impacts of these different lifestyles. Throwing away edible food means wasting all of the energy and resources that brought it to your plate. Britons throw away 12 per cent of edible food. If you were on an average diet this would be 240 carbos – as much as two Mediterranean railway holidays. And once the food waste is in the landfill it rots, producing yet more of that deadly methane. That's another 100 kg (220 lb) of carbon dioxide.

5 Transport emissions are serious

Why does the UK import 126 million litres (222 million pints) of milk from the continent and then export 270 million litres (475 million pints)? It doesn't make sense. Maybe the milk is being put in the bottles abroad and then returned. It is quite possible. I once hitched a lift from a lorry that was carrying Belgian potatoes to Italy to be washed before taking them back to be packed.

And buying green beans flown from Kenya really does seem extraordinarily decadent – the kind of thing that our grandchildren will sneer at in their history classes. In his book *How to Live a Low Carbon Life*, Chris Goodall calculates that a single pack of spinach flown from the US produced 1 kg (2.2 lb) of carbon dioxide. As he says, it only takes 15 bags of this spinach to equal the entire annual carbon emissions of a person in Afghanistan.

All in all, the road transportation of food accounts for 240 carbos per person on an average diet. Air freight is somewhat less, just over 30 carbos on average, but it could be far higher for some people.

Chapter 6
What you buy
Goods and services

So far this carbo count has been relatively straightforward because the figures are easy to find. However, when we start looking at the goods and services we buy it all becomes far more complex.

A pair of woollen socks, for example, contains a share of the emissions produced by the sheep (which, as we know, are a climate menace). The wool is then processed, turned to yarn, knitted, cut, packaged and finally sold to you. The socks contain a share of the emissions of every factory, warehouse and shop in this process, not to mention the transport that is needed at every stage.

And this is just for socks. Every factory, shop and office is using energy and contributing to emissions. Across the whole UK economy, manufacturing and services account for a third of all emissions, and finding out which part is your share is as hard as finding out the exact source of the rain that ends up coming out of your tap.

However, as someone who wants to live light and leave no stone unturned in your quest to mix your metaphors, you will not want to skate over a corner of your life that probably accounts for a quarter of your total climate impact.

So we will try to estimate the spending emissions using a rough rule of thumb; we will assume that, having allowed for your spending on home heating, transport and food, we can give a standard carbo value to each remaining pound that you spend on new goods and services. In the appendices I explain how I reached this value (see pages 333–4).

The quick-and-easy version

As usual, only use this easy carbo-counter if you are in a hurry. Otherwise go on to the fancy version on pages 222–3.

After I have paid my rent, mortgage, tax, food, travel, flights and everything already talked about, my remaining disposable spending money is:

	Carbos
Under £50 a week	1,000
For every additional £50 spending money	add 1,000
Buying subtotal	

Now divide this by the number of people you are directly supporting

Total consumption emissions per person

Enter this figure in row 6 of the table on page 227

The fancy version

As with all of the fancy versions, there are a few questions that need answering before you begin.

Where do I find the figures?

You need to find your take-home salary and get some idea of where your spending is going. You could guess it, but you might also like to go through some bank statements to find the proportions. I suggest that you start by removing your regular expenditure on food, petrol, utilities, rent and council tax before breaking your remaining spending into the zero, light, standard and heavy carbo bands on the counter.

What about my rent or mortgage?

I have decided to exclude rents and mortgages from the calculation and divide the emissions of new buildings equally between everyone.

Although there are very substantial emissions involved in the building of a new house, it doesn't seem fair that they should all be charged to the first person to move in when the house is likely to stand for at least a hundred years and be used by many other people. New houses are a small part of the total UK housing stock, and the vast majority of rent and mortgage spending is just a financial transfer for houses that have already been built. For both these reasons I ask you to remove your rent and mortgage payments before doing the counter.

What about imports?

I am assuming that the emissions produced by the things we import are balanced by the emissions produced by the things we export. This may well not be true – after all, a lot of heavy industry has moved to the growing economies of Asia. However, it would be impossible to allow for where goods come from in the calculations (most likely a car has come from a dozen different countries) so we stick to the rough rule of thumb.

What about my spending on holiday?

As with imports, I am assuming that money you spend abroad is balanced by spending by a visitor in the UK. So, yes, you should include it.

My car was second-hand. That's zero emissions, right?

You've got to be joking! A car is the most energy-intensive product you own and you have already been charged 300 carbos a year for it. Cars are owned by a chain of people and each one of them pays a market price that is based on the assumption that he or she will be able to sell it later. It is only fair that everyone in the chain pays for the emissions that went into making it.

Buying things

Step 1: Disposable income

Start with your net take-home salary after income tax, then deduct

- Council taxes
- Rent or mortgage payments
- Your power utility bills
- Personal travel costs
- Spending on food
- Payments for the purchase of a car
- Money that you give away to friends and family but not to general charities

Now also remove all spending on goods and services that make a positive contribution to climate change. We shall treat these as 'zero rated' for carbo purposes

- Investments in the light-carbon economy, such as renewables
- Personal donations to organizations working to prevent climate change, improve energy efficiency or promote renewable energy
- Payments to offset companies or organizations

Your total net annual disposable income for general consumption of general goods and services is

Step 2: Light carbo spending

These are goods and services that produce low emissions as a proportion of the total cost

- Second-hand goods, clothes and antiques
- Labour-intensive products – for example, bespoke furniture, arts and crafts, tailor-made clothing, musical instruments
- Personal labour-based services – for example, childcare, cleaners, gardeners and decorators

Multiply your spending on light-carbo goods and products by 0.1

Step 3: Heavy carbo spending

These are manufactured products that have high inputs of materials and energy – for example, computers, electronics and household goods, like refrigerators and washing machines.

Multiply your spending on heavy-carbo goods and products by 1

Step 4: Standard carbo spending

These are all the other services and goods you buy. Unless you keep your money sown into the mattress, the money you save also counts as standard spending as it is being reinvested and will produce emissions elsewhere in the economy.

Add together steps 2 and 3 and deduct them from your disposable income in step 1 to find your standard carbo spending.

Multiply this by 0.4 to give your total standard spending carbos

Step 5: Your spending carbos

Add together steps 2, 3 and 4 and divide by the number of people you support to get your personal consumption emissions

Enter this figure in row 6 of the table on page 227

Carbo lessons

1 Rich people have higher emissions than poor people

Yes, it stands to reason. If you are a living in a small flat and eking out a state pension you will probably already be living pretty light. If you have a large income you are likely to have higher emissions even if you avoid the big-ticket items like flights. Your challenge is to shift your spending into the lower carbo areas.

2 There are very large differences between light carbo spending and standard carbo spending

I have calculated light carbo spending at one-quarter of the impact of standard carbo spending, and, if anything, this is probably still too high. After all, the emissions involved in driving junk to a car-boot sale or running a charity shop don't even begin to compare with those of making something new.

There are many personal services in which the large majority of the cost is labour. A cleaner, gardener or decorator, for example, may use some materials, but these are still a very small part of the total cost.

3 Buying second-hand things only saves emissions as part of a light-carbon lifestyle

Buying something second-hand has far lower emissions? Yes, that is indeed true. However, buying something second-hand is usually a lot cheaper too, so it leaves you with more money to spend on something else.

Take clothes, for example. Everything I am wearing as I

type this chapter is second-hand, apart from socks, underwear and a jumper that my mum gave me for Christmas (and thankfully didn't knit herself). I spent £50 at charity shops and car-boot sales on an ensemble that would have cost me £200 new. Although the £50 accounts for only five carbos, the savings I made by buying second-hand have freed £150 for other spending. If that went into travel or high carbo spending the end result would be worse for the climate. Second-hand living really pays off when it is part of a lower-earning lifestyle (see Earn light, page 273).

4 Offset companies are only zero carbo spending not 'carbon neutral'

Offset companies say that, for a low fee, they will fund projects that reduce emissions. Excellent – I'm all in favour, and for this reason payments to offset companies are zero rated. However, I do not agree with the marketing claim that offsets can make you 'carbon neutral'. We have a responsibility for our own emissions, and our goal should be to find a better way to live. You can't detox your carbon by paying someone else to do it for you any more than you can detox your liver by paying someone to stay at home while you go to the pub.

Nor do I accept that personal offsetting is paving the way for a new light-carbon economy. A while ago I sat at lunch next to an Oxford economist who is a senior advisor to Sir Nicholas Stern (we met his report on pages 106–107) and lectures around the world about the devastating economic impacts of climate change. Considering that he is already jetting everywhere for his work I asked him if he flew for personal reasons. Oh yes, he said, he flew often and had just had a very pleasant holiday in South Africa. In response to my choking noises he argued that it was OK because he 'offset' his flights. He said that by doing this he was helping to establish a higher market price for carbon, which, he believed, was crucial for sending a clear market signal to polluters. In his view, it was far better to engage actively in the carbon market than to stay at home.

It all sounded very logical and persuasive. But what it was really proving was that really clever people can build really clever arguments for doing what they want to do anyway. It is true that buying an offset sends a market signal that says:

'Please can we value carbon higher,'

but paying £600 for a return flight to South Africa sends a much louder market signal:

'Give me lots more long haul jet trips.'

If we are serious about this detox we need to factor in all our actions the kind of world we would like to see not the one that we think we can get away with. By all means make donations to organizations that are reducing emissions, but don't let that take away your determination to address the real root causes of your own emissions.

Chapter 7

Counting the carbos
Your total

And now it's time to tot up all your totals and find out how you compare with the average Briton.

Write in all your carbos from the six steps

	Carbos for you	Carbos for average UK person
1 House		2,900
2 Car		1,300
3 Public transport		190
4 Flights		1,830
5 Food		2,000
6 Goods and services		3,310
Your total carbos		11,530

To this we have to add the emissions produced by the government on behalf of all of us. Whatever the taxes you pay or the personal use you make of these services, they still count equally for your final total.

7 Government services	1,000	1,000
Your carbon bottom line		12,530

Chapter 8

What does it all mean?
What is the acceptable carbo target?

You remember that each 'carbo' is the *equivalent* of 1 kg (2.2 lb) of carbon dioxide? So, 1,000 carbos are the *equivalent* of 1 tonne of carbon dioxide. Now you know how many kilos or tonnes you are producing and can see how you compare with the UK average.

But knowing this still doesn't get you any closer to understanding what that means. A tonne of carbon dioxide is a huge volume of gas, but even if I told you how many balloons it would fill you would still be no closer to understanding the climate impact.

It is a bit like being told that you are eating 6,000 calories a day: it doesn't mean anything. What is a calorie anyway? What you need is a target. If I told you that someone your size should only be eating 3,000 calories a day you would soon understand how you got so chunky.

So we need to find a target

The British government's target is to reduce emissions by 60 per cent by 2050. So, by 2050 we will all have to be down to an average of 5,000 carbos. Now how are you doing? Are you there yet? As you can see this is a challenging target.

And unfortunately, it is still far too high. As I will explain we will need to go far further unless we intend to keep the majority of the world's people in permanent poverty in order to subsidize our lifestyles.

Let's start from first principles. The forests, soils and oceans permanently remove around 10 billion tonnes of carbon dioxide (and equivalent) from the atmosphere each year. So, if we can keep total global emissions at this level we can stabilize the atmospheric concentrations and, in time, stabilize global temperatures.

The challenge is finding a way to divide up that total allowance of 10 billion tonnes. One way to do this would be to auction it off to the highest bidder. The developing countries have total emissions of 6 billion tonnes. If we prevent them from ever increasing their emissions further that will leave the rich countries fighting over the remaining 8 billion tonnes. We currently emit 18 billion tonnes, so we will have to reduce by 60 per cent – the current government target – which brings us back to 4,500 carbos.

However, if we reduce our emissions by only 60 per cent we will have to deny three-quarters of the world's population any chance of increasing theirs. Considering that, in large areas of Africa and Asia, people are living on scarcely £1 or £2 a day I find this utterly appalling. This may be how things work out – it is, after all, how we usually do things, but maintaining it will require that we create and enforce a permanent structure of inequality – a carbon apartheid.

And I don't think that we will ever be able to get away with that. There are two emerging superpowers among those developing countries – India and China – and I see no way that they will stall their own surging economies in order to give us a softer landing. We need an international agreement, and we will never get one on these terms.

So the only other option requires us to make deeper cuts in our emissions in order to allow developing countries some room to expand theirs. If we divided up the total allowance of 10 billion tonnes equally among the 7 billion people in the world that would give us a new target of 1.5 tonnes each – just 1,500 carbos. This requires that we reduce our emissions by 87 per cent by 2050, and, if the world population keeps increasing, by even more. This proposal, called Contraction and Convergence, has many powerful supporters. Like them I believe that it is the only just and politically feasible option.

Whatever happens in the intense and aggressive political horse-trading of the next few years, everyone in Britain is going to have to reduce his or her carbon to somewhere between 1,500 and 4,500 carbos. Your long-term target for a full carbon detox needs to be within this range.

Chapter 9

The bottom line

Four steps to a full carbon detox

In the last chapter we found that the target for a full detox will be just 1½ carbo tonnes. You can't get there all at once, but you can commit yourself to some goals to get you on the way.

• Step 1: I will reduce my emissions to below the UK average in every category.

• Step 2: I will reduce my total emissions by at least 1 tonne (1,000 carbos) per year.

• Step 3: I will aim to reduce my total carbo bottom line to 4 tonnes (4,000 carbos) per year.

• Step 4: My long-term, lifetime goal is to reduce all of my emissions to 1½ tonnes (1,500 carbos) per year.

Step 1 is entirely reasonable, isn't it? The average Briton's emissions are three to six times higher than any long-term target. The very least we can do is to reach that average.

Step 2 is based on a fully achievable detox programme that I know you can do in a year. In the section that follows

I show you exactly how you can drop a carbo tonne in any area of your life.

Step 3 is a realistic final goal in our heavy-carbon culture. Your personal carbos are all of the ones you have control over – your house, your transport and the things you buy. You will still be some way off the 1½-tonne target and the government will still be producing emissions that you have no control over, but it is a very good and impressive start and certainly deserves full recognition. Do this and you can certainly consider yourself pretty well detoxed.

Step 4 is where, ultimately, you have to get to. However, emissions of 1½ tonnes per person are not yet possible in Britain – the government has burned up half that much on your behalf before you even turn on your kettle. In the longer term the government will start to grapple with its own emissions, and this target will become much more realistic and attainable.

So, now you have some goals, how did you do? Did you look at your results and think: 'I should be writing this book.' Great, off you go then – call the publishers. Maybe you thought, 'Oh my god, we're all doomed.' If you did, I fear you have a very pessimistic view of people's capacity to change.

I hope that, being a reasonably positive person, your response has been: OK, I now see how hard this is, but I also understand much better which areas are really problematic and that if we can rethink and change the choices we make we are most of the way there. I hope, though, that you also recognize that the real obstacle in making these changes is believing in the problem and that we have the power to change it.

Let's consider your results

My total and all my boxes are above the UK average

Oh dear. The first goal has to be to get all of these below the UK average. You can start by picking out the two categories that are highest and concentrate your actions on these. For most people the big-ticket items will most likely relate to travel – either long-distance flights or commuting.

My total is below average but some of my boxes are still above average

You are starting to move in the right direction. What you should do now is focus your attention on the boxes that are above average. UK average emissions are far too high in all respects, so you need to get these down. Once all your boxes are below average you can start to choose the ones you want to work on further.

My total and all my boxes are below average

Now you are really starting to live light. You are ready to move on to step 2 and aim to drop a tonne a year. I recommend focusing on a few big-ticket items and dealing with them thoroughly. Alternatively, you can pick out a couple of areas for special attention – such as a DIY weekend to deal thoroughly with your house.

My total is already below 6 tonnes

You are indeed a 21st-century citizen. Congratulations. You will now find it hard to drop a tonne through any single big-ticket item. This is the point at which you should be looking thoroughly at every aspect of your life to find areas where you can trim further. Although I have been sarcastic about the thousands of tips in articles and 'save the planet' books, you will find ideas and inspiration in there to achieve these further incremental stages. You could also consider ways to publicize what you are doing – such as becoming an 'amplifier' (see pages 297–9).

My total is already under 5 tonnes

Wow. You have really embraced and accepted the challenge of light living. Well done. You are living proof that a light-carbon life can be rich, satisfying and fun. Why do we think that we can't do anything about climate change when there are people like you around? I suggest that you should now concentrate on the advanced strategies – 'taking control' (see pages 294–6) and 'amplifying' (see pages 297–9).

OK everyone, please humour me and fill in the personal pledge opposite

My target for this coming year is to reduce my overall carbon
emissions to _____ units

I will concentrate my action on two areas:

1 _____

_____

_____

_____

_____

_____

_____

2 _____

_____

_____

_____

_____

_____

And now let's look at some of the ways that you can not only
meet this target, but beat it.

Part 9
Drop a tonne

Chapter 1

Drop a tonne at home
The big-ticket items

Dropping a tonne on home power requires reducing the energy consumption of an average British house by a quarter. This is completely possible. I know, because I have managed to reduce energy consumption in my own modest house by two-thirds.

If you live in a large house or use electricity for heating you should be able to drop more than a tonne. Whether this reduces your personal emissions by a tonne will depend on how many people you live with, so you may want to combine several options to make it up to a tonne per person.

Insulate a cavity wall
Drops 1–2 tonnes

It is daft not to insulate a cavity wall if you have one, which is very likely if your house was built after 1920. The insulation installer can tell you if you have one or not. He then drills a hole in the wall and pumps foam into the cavity. In the past there were health concerns about chemicals released from the foam, but it is now quite safe and stable. And it is cheap as chips. There are a number of heavily subsidized deals available and it will usually cost around

£150 for a semi-detached house. This will pay for itself within 18 months or sooner. If you are on pension or benefits you may well be eligible for free installation through the Warmfront programme.

Action: Call your local Energy Advice Centre.

Replace electric heating with gas central heating

Drops between 3 and 10 tonnes

As we found in the last section, electric heating is a heavy-carbo item because only a third of the energy ever reaches you. Replacing electric heating will be expensive – around £2,000 – but it will save you several hundred pounds a year, and if you own your house or are a landlord it is an investment that will go straight onto the value of the house.

Action: Call plumbers for quotes.

Insulate an uninsulated loft as thickly as you can

Drops 1.5 tonnes or more

This is an easy and obvious saving. There are a wide number of subsidized schemes available that will do this for around £150 or for free if you are eligible for benefits. If you have old, thin insulation that has shrunk away from the joists and is weighed down by dust it may well be next to useless, and you could drop a tonne by replacing it. So how thick can it be? Well obviously, because each additional layer saves less energy than the last but takes just as much energy to make, there is point at which further insulation is a waste of time. For rock wool (the pink fluffy stuff) this is 1 metre (3 feet). The standard advice is to insulate to a depth of 27 cm (10½ in), and builders and DIY installers meet this figure with exactitude. As usual with insulation standards, the bar is set absurdly low and the real advice should be 'whack in as much as you possible can'.

Action: Call your local Energy Advice Centre or go and buy a few rolls (and a face mask) and install your own.

Replace electrical water heating with a solar panel

Drops 1.2 tonnes

Solar hot water is the cheapest and most effective of the renewables and hopefully will become a standard feature of all houses. It is still quite expensive though: a typical installation costs around £3,000. It will save over a tonne if you are replacing electrical heating, but only half a tonne if you are replacing gas.

Action: Find a reputable local installer who is a member of the Solar Trade Association.

Heat with wood

Drops anything from 1 to 5 tonnes

In theory, wood is a zero-emission fuel. However, to drop the full tonne you must use a good-quality modern burner that meets air regulations. The sooty particulates in wood smoke from an open fire or poor-quality burner produce serious local air pollution and have a global warming impact that can outweigh the gains from using wood.

The cheapest option is to install a wood burner in an existing fireplace as a supplement to the existing heating system. This will cost around £1,000, and you can get a government grant for up to 20 per cent. If used regularly in the winter this will drop the full tonne. If you want to go the whole hog you can install a wood-fired boiler that will heat your whole house. Boiler and installation costs from £3,000 to £5,000 but there are government grants for up to 30 per cent of the cost. If you are clever, you can run it on free waste wood, such as pallets, or there are wood-pellet models that are more expensive to run but save you the trouble of constantly loading the fire.

Action: Look at www.lowcarbonbuildings.org.uk for grants and ideas.

Switch to renewable electricity

Drops 1.5 to 3 tonnes

Buying electricity from a renewable electricity company will remove virtually all of your electricity emissions. Yes, there are emissions involved in building windmills and dams, but these are usually no more than a few per cent of the emissions saved. Be careful to choose a good company: some are simply charging extra for renewable energy that the power companies are legally obliged to produce anyway.

Action: Shop around for suppliers and tariffs.

Fill a spare room

Drops up to 4 tonnes

Finally, the single step that makes the greatest difference: get a lodger or housemate. Nothing else achieves emissions reductions faster and makes more money for you. Renting out an empty room can earn you £2,500 a year or more, the house will be more secure, and you will have someone new to talk to. Choose a lodger well and you may find a friend for life. (My old landlady Fran is now godmother to my daughter. We call her the Grandlady.)

Action: Contact your local authority housing department and ask for advice about letting a room.

Finally, there are two major measures that are outside the realms of the usual DIY enthusiast, but that are completely worth doing as part of an overall energy strategy.

Fit thermostatic radiator valves (TRVs) on all radiators

Drops half a tonne or more

TRVs sit on the in-valve on your radiator and switch off the radiator when the room has reached a chosen temperature. They are very useful devices and an invaluable part of the energy-saving kit. Unless you are a competent home plumber you had better get a professional to fit them, so call around for a quote or wait until you need another plumbing job done and get them done then. They will cost about £15 each, and the installation should be relatively quick. But, as I say below, they will realize their full saving only if you use them properly.

Action: Call plumbers for quotes for the job. Make sure you combine it with another plumbing job.

Install top-quality heating controls

Drops three-quarters of a tonne

Modern heating controls are far more clever than a timer and thermostat. They can vary temperatures precisely throughout the day and allow for delays in the rate at which a house heats up. They cost around £200 and can be installed easily, although you should bring in an electrician for this job. The Energy Savings Trust argues that good heating controls are the most cost-effective way of saving energy after insulation. But, like TRVs, you have to know how to use them and, as discussed later on, you have to tweak them.

Action: Call electricians for quotes.

And what about all those things that are missing from this list?

Double glazing

The energy savings of double glazing are surprisingly poor considering the cost. It is worth installing once you have done all other insulation and draught-proofing. Incidentally, in an existing house you will save more energy – and a lot more money – if you fit secondary internal glazing rather than replacing the outside windows.

Photovoltaic panels

Solar electricity panels on your roof *will* drop a tonne or more. But they will also cost you dearly: at least £10,000, although there are government grants for up to half of this. These are high-technology items that come with a lot of wires and controls, so if you are a techno-head and that appeals to you, then by all means go for it. For most people, though, I recommend doing everything else first.

Wind turbines

You can now buy small, domestic, roof wind turbines for £1,000 upwards. If you have unbroken exposure to wind – for example, you live on the hill facing the coast – they may make sense. Sadly, they make little sense on houses in built-up areas and really don't produce much power. They are fun and look great, so by all means get one if that excites you.

Appliances

There has been a transformation in the performance of electrical appliances over the last ten years. If you replace a

1990s appliance with a new A or A+ energy rated model, each year you will save 230 carbos for a freezer, 160 for a dishwasher, 105 carbos for a refrigerator and 60 carbos for a washing machine. As these figures show, you would have to replace every appliance to drop a whole tonne, so I advise you to feel happy and confident about replacing older appliances, even if they are working fine, but don't let that distract you from the cheaper big-ticket items.

Many of these actions are expensive and need careful planning and saving. For a full carbon detox you will have to do them. However, in the next chapter we will find a whole set of smaller and cheaper measures with which you can drop your first tonne. Many appear on the 'easy things to do' lists, but actually they are not so easy. To get the full saving and get them done you will have to block out the time to do them – for example as a DIY weekend.

Chapter 2

The DIY weekend to drop a tonne

Getting the fiddly things done at once

There are a number of small measures that are easy to do, that will drop a tonne or more and that will make your home much more comfortable. Because they are all small and fiddly we never get round to them, so the trick is to bulk them up and do them all in one weekend. So block out your DIY weekend to do as many of the following as possible.

Change *every* lightbulb

Drops 20 carbos per bulb – a third of a tonne for an average house

Replace every incandescent or halogen to a low-energy or LED bulb (see page 170 for more details). Yes, *all* of them. There are no good excuses for not doing this. It is not true that they take lots of energy to warm up. It is not true that you can't find low-energy replacements for dimmers or spotlights – specialist lighting suppliers on the Internet have low-energy bulbs for every fitting. Halogen spotlights, I have to tell you, glug energy and should be a priority for replacement. And if you say, 'I don't like the colour of the light', you are just making excuses.

Draught-proof every leaky door and window and around the hatch to the attic
Drops 100 carbos or more
Fit draught-proofing strip around all windows and external doors, fit brushes under external doors and doors leading into a cold hallway and the attic hatch.

Seal gaps under skirting boards and between floorboards on the ground floor
Drops 100 carbos
Gaps can be a major source of draughts in an older house that has a cellar or a ventilated void under the ground floor. You can fill them with slivers of insulation and mastic.

Lag all accessible hot water pipes
Drops 50 carbos
Every time you run the hot water tap you waste the heat in the pipe that runs from the tank or boiler. Pipe insulation is cheap and easy to fit, but remember to check the diameter of your pipes before going to the shop. Don't bother insulating central heating pipes.

Insulate your hot water tank properly
Drops 120 carbos
Remember you can fit 1 metre (3 feet) of insulation before

you are wasting your time, so even if your tank already has some insulation, you should fit as much as you possibly can. You can buy tank insulation jackets at most DIY stores, but I don't rate them much. They are usually flimsy and badly made. I recommend doing it yourself by wrapping good second-hand insulation materials around the tank – duvets, blankets or sheets of bubble wrap are ideal – and holding them tight with a few cordons of strong duct tape. If your tank is boxed into a cupboard, you can pack in stuff all around it. Be careful to leave some access to the tank thermostat – you will need to tweak it (see pages 256–7).

Fit insulating reflective foil behind radiators sitting on external walls

Drops 100 carbos

Most DIY stores sell rolls of reflective insulation for taping behind radiators to reflect heat away from the wall. Radiators on internal walls are fine as they are.

Defrost freezer and dust freezer and fridge coils

Drops 20 carbos

Even though these are good basic maintenance jobs they are easy to forget. A third of people never do either and wonder why their freezer packs in.

Turn radiators down or off, adjust thermostats and start tweaking

Drops half a tonne or more

In the next chapter I give a range of 'below the line' changes to your domestic heating system. All of them will add up significantly.

Fit short extensions and new socket strips to make power switches accessible

Drop 25 carbos

The trick to turning things off standby is making access as easy as possible. If you switch a TV, video and digital box off standby you will save 60 kilowatt hours altogether, which is 25 carbos. This is worth doing, but it is still a very small saving and it is astonishing how often we are told that turning things off standby is a major solution to climate change.

Action points for your DIY weekend

1 Pick a buddy if you can and decide to help each other out.
2 Choose a weekend and write it in the calendar.
3 Write a shopping list and buy everything you need well ahead of time. You should be able to get much of what you need at the DIY chain stores. Lightbulbs can also be bought on the Internet and from IKEA, which has a very wide range of energy-saving bulbs (though not LEDs). You can buy very cheap old duvets, jumpers and blankets for insulating the water tank at car-boot sales.
4 Keep the weekend clear and do it.

Now we will look at the crucial missing component: the detox attitude. You should be able to drop a tonne by changing your behaviour. It will take a week and it won't cost you a penny.

Chapter 3

Drop a tonne on home power
Unfreeze your habits

Many of the ways in which we use energy at home are habitual. We don't really know how many lights we turn on because we rarely think about it. We don't choose a temperature for the house – we simply get used to whatever the heating system decides to give us. In cold houses we put on a jumper, and in warm houses we sit around in our underpants.

I don't want you to think all the time about your heating or lighting or how much water you put in the kettle. Life is too short to be filled with such pettiness. What I *do* want you to do is to examine each of your habits, unfreeze it, try something lighter and then make that your new way of doing things.

Adapt what you do already

Remember all those energy-saving habits that are so habitual that you don't even think about them? What we need to do is to extend those habits to include new patterns that, once they are absorbed, will take no effort, time or money. Here are some simple everyday habits with adaptations. How painful do any of them sound? None of them would change you in any way, and, once they are habitual, you won't even notice that you are doing them.

Current living	Light living
✗ Turn off lights when you go to bed	✓ Turn off lights when you leave the room
✗ Turn off the heating when you go on holiday	✓ Turn off the heating when you leave the house
✗ Turn off the TV when you go to bed	✓ Turn off everything at the wall when you go to bed
✗ Turn off the shower when you get out	✓ Turn off the shower while you lather your hair or shave
✗ Close the front door when you leave the house	✓ Close the front door when you go out in the garden or chat in the road

Unfreezing day

All I ask for is **one** day on which you adapt what you do and unfreeze your habits. Do this with a friend or a partner so that you can compare notes and have a laugh about it. Start by picking a typical day, ideally in the winter when you are heating the house.

During your unfreezing day I want you to treat energy as though it were the most precious and rare commodity on earth. I want you to give your heating and washing energy as much attention as the women in dry parts of Africa who have to walk for two hours in the blazing sun to collect a bundle of twigs for fuel wood. I want you to think of water as though you had to walk another two hours in the other direction to the well and then carry it back on your head. You will:

• Turn the tap on and off for exactly the amount you need.

• Rinse dishes under the cold tap.

• Learn exactly how much water to put in the kettle and practise getting it right.

• Turn off the oven and things boiling on the stove five minutes before you need them and let them cook in the residual heat.

• Turn down the house thermostat to 18°C (64.5°F).

• Take control of the heating. Leave it off and only turn it on when you feel cold. As soon as you feel warm, turn it off again.

• Turn off the heating an hour before you leave the house and an hour before you go to bed.

• Turn off all electrical appliances, especially computers and televisions, as soon as you have finished using them.

• Turn off every light when you leave a room.

• Turn off the shower when you are soaping yourself, shampooing your hair or shaving.

• Plan ahead and defrost frozen food overnight in the fridge.

• Run a washing machine or dishwasher* only when it is full and only on the lowest economy setting.

• Hang all clothes to dry.

By the end of unfreezing day you will certainly have used a lot less energy. Three of my friends tried an unfreezing day and they found that they used a quarter less energy. If they lived like that all the time, they would drop a tonne and a half off their house emissions.

With your partner or friend, consider which things felt hard and inconvenient and which seemed easy. On the next day stick with the easy things and see if you can keep them going for a whole week. Within a few days you will not even notice that you are doing them any more, and by the end of the week you would be well on the way to doing them permanently.

Of these various measures the ones that drop the most carbos are those concerned with the house heating. Every time you turn the average boiler off for an hour you drop four carbos. If you could do that every day for a whole heating season you would have painlessly dropped over 500 carbos. Combine this with other measures and you will knock off the whole tonne.

And if it seems like a pain, just remember how much work our grandparents had carrying coal, building fires and

*I am strongly convinced that dishwashers use less energy than hand washing. However, if you disagree wash the dishes in the sink during unfreezing day.

cleaning up the mess? Surely it is not too much trouble to take control over the heating if you have a wall thermostat that you can simply turn on and off. How long does that take? A few seconds? All I am asking for is a few seconds of thought a day.

The real trick to dropping carbos is anticipating when to turn the heating off. A reasonably insulated house will keep its heat for a while, so try turning off the heat an hour before you leave the house. This could be part of a routine – for example, turning it off just before breakfast or just after the TV evening news. And you absolutely must turn it off when you leave the house, so have a reminder note by the door.

Finally, now that are really thinking detox you can have a little fiddle with your house that could very well drop tonnes. Get ready to tweak.

Chapter 4

Tweak a tonne
Play with your knobs (girls too)

The average house is full of controls and thermostats. There is a house thermostat, room thermostats, radiator thermostats, boiler-flow thermostats and hot water thermostats. And then there are timers and numerous overrides. That's a lot of things pushing and pulling your heating system in different directions.

Is it any surprise, then, that many systems are completely out of balance? Heating comes on too early or too late; radiators are too hot in one place, too cold in another; water is heated at the wrong time of day to the wrong temperature.

What you need to do is carefully balance your heating to give you precisely what you want when you want it – no more, no less. And the way you achieve that is by entering a period of careful tweaking

So this is what you do

You start with everything at a generous setting. Then, at a designated time each week you take everything down just a little. If it feels fine then the next week you tweak it down a little more. If anything feels too cool, you know you have reached the limit and you can just tweak it up a little before leaving it. A few weeks of this and your whole house will be balanced.

Why do I think that men might go for this? You know how you like to read manuals and fiddle with things. You like to tinker with engines or twitch your amp settings. I think this is right up your street.

Start by tweaking the radiators. Turn off radiators in any rooms that are rarely used – you can always turn the radiator back on if you need to. In all transit spaces, such as corridors and hallways, radiators should be turned way down and, ideally, off. Hallways are a major place for heat loss, so you want them to be unheated. It will also make your heated rooms *feel* warmer and more inviting when you enter from a cooler space. If you don't believe me, try it and see.

If you have thermostatic radiator valves you can now carefully adjust the remaining radiators. The settings on the dial are usually not very reliable, so I suggest starting with a setting just over halfway and edging it down little by little until you find the right setting for the room temperature you want. Avoid the temptation to fiddle with them afterwards. I recommend a target temperature of 20°C (68°F) for a bathroom and 16°C (61°F) for bedrooms. This, incidentally, is now the recommended bedroom temperature for small babies.

At the same time, reduce the boiler flow temperature. There is usually a dial on the side of the boiler, so see what happens with it set to halfway round. One reason for doing this is that boilers tend to be more efficient at lower temperatures, especially condensing boilers. But an even better reason is that a house will feel warmer if the radiators are on as long as possible and the best way to achieve this is to run them at a lower temperature.

Once you have balanced the radiators, tweak the main house thermostat. If you are used to a very warm house start with a thermostat set to 20°C (68°F) and just edge it down half a degree a week until it feels right. I find 18°C (64.5°F) perfect in my house, but every house is different. If you have a fancy, all-bangs-and-whistles thermostat you can give it different temperature settings throughout the day. I suggest that the temperature during the evening is a degree or two higher than during daylight. If your house thermostat is in the hall (where you have probably turned off the heating) you will be taking the setting much further down, although I would recommend getting an electrician to move it into your living room.

If you have a hot water tank it will have a thermostat – usually a small box on the side or a control box on the wall. There is absolutely no point having a tank full of water at 80°C (176°F), which scalds you when it comes out the tap, so tweak it down until you have the water at just the right temperature that a full tank can meet your needs. Hot bath water is only around 40°C (104°F), so if you have a large enough tank it doesn't need to be much hotter than that. Once you have got it right, lag the tank. If you have a combination boiler, set the hot water thermostat in the mid-range. It should not need further tweaking.

And finally, there are the timers. Automatic timers are a menace because people set them and then never touch them again. I have one friend whose house got unbearably hot in the middle of the night. He hadn't noticed that the timer had once stopped during a power cut and had been out of sync ever since. So set the heating timer to turn on an hour before you get up and end when you go to bed and then tweak it to start later and end earlier. And don't forget to turn it all off when you go out.

Set the water timer to run for an hour twice a day, with the first time slot starting at the same time as the house heating (this will put a good load on the boiler). And trim them back by a couple of minutes at a time.

And why am I suggesting you do all of this? It all sounds a bit petty doesn't it, but you know I wouldn't take up your time if I didn't think that the carbo savings would be high

Look at it this way. The average outside temperature between October and April is 11.5°C (53°F). You already have a couple of degrees of waste heat in the house from cooking, electrics and body heat, and all your heating system is doing it topping it up to your desired living temperature. If you want 18°C (64.5°F) you will need an extra 4.5°C (8°F) of heat. However, if you want 21°C (70°F) you will need an extra 7.5°C (13.5°F) of heat. That is a huge amount more heating for a few extra degrees.

In an average house if you tweak as I suggest and get your heating levels down a couple of degrees overall, you will drop at least a tonne. I guarantee it. A cooler house is fresher, healthier and will make you feel livelier. And you will be living a lot lighter without any cost, major work or loss in comfort.

Chapter 5

Drop a tonne on land travel

Cutting down on car emissions

There are huge discrepancies between people's travel emissions. One person may walk to work and go on holiday by train. Another will go everywhere by car and commute long distances to work. The difference between the two could be several tonnes.

So you may be able to drop several tonnes on land or none at all – it will all depend on your starting point. If you have some serious travel emissions all of the following will drop a tonne exactly.

Drop 4,800 kilometres (3,000 miles) off your annual mileage

If you have an average-sized car, you will drop a tonne if you can transfer 4,800 kilometres (3,000 miles) of your annual mileage to public transport. Now, before you start reckoning that this is some vast distance, just break it down across a year and you will see it is not so much. Many of us do regular journeys that add up to 4,800 kilometres (3,000 miles) in a year. Maybe you drive 200 kilometres (125 miles) each way once a month to visit your granny, or 50 kilometres (30 miles) each way once a week to visit your mum or boyfriend. That's easily 4,800 kilometres (3,000 miles). And a daily commute of just 10 kilometres (6 miles) each way clocks up that much. Wouldn't you prefer to be sitting on a chauffeur-driven bus reading the paper or listening to music?

Work from home one day a week

If you have a car commute to work of 50 kilometres (30 miles) or more each way, you will drop a tonne if you are able to work from home one day a week. You will probably get more work done anyway. The same is true for a round-trip rail commute of 275 kilometres (170 miles).

Share other people's toys

The best way to halve the fuel consumption of a car is to share it. You get company for the ride and someone who can pay your petrol. Of course, there are inconveniences too. You will have to agree when to go and, although you might not admit it, you probably don't like the idea of sharing your toys. So how about offering to share the petrol costs of someone else's car? That way you get chauffeur driven and it's their car that gets the wear and tear. Sharing is especially sensible for commuting. You will drop a tonne if your daily commute is more than 18 kilometres (11 miles) each way.

Get a new car

Generally speaking, your best option is to switch to a diesel engine. If you drive more than 12,800 kilometres (8,000 miles) a year you will drop a tonne simply by switching from a petrol car to a diesel version of the same model. And if you have a diesel, you have all the options of using vegetable-based fuels too.

You may have heard a lot of talk about hybrids – the latest development in car technology – that combine a petrol engine for long journeys with an electric engine for town travel. Many Hollywood stars have them, and I understand that they are great to drive. In terms of the carbon bottom line, though, there are diesel cars that are nearly as good. The Toyota Prius Hybrid, for example, does 9.6 kilometres (6 miles) to the carbo. The diesel-powered Citroen C1 or Toyota Aygo will do 9.1 kilometres (5.6 miles) to the carbo. There really isn't much in it. Even the Ford Fiesta diesel does 8.6 kilometres (5.3 miles) to the carbo.

Live close to work (or work close to home)

Commuting is, as we have seen already, a huge cause of transport carbos and a total waste of your life. Do you spend hours every week jammed into the corner of a railway carriage or stuck in traffic? Could you avoid commuting all together?

This is my commute to work. I leave the house at 8.45 a.m., cycle along a tree-lined path by the nature reserve. I then cut up past the supermarket (handy for last-minute shopping on the way home), across a large park and down to the office. I arrive fresh, energized and a little fitter.

There was no luck or special privilege required to live like this. I can have this joyful commute because I gave a very high priority to living close to work. I could have a fancier house if I lived out of town. I could have a much higher salary if I was prepared to work in London. So there is a clear trade-off. But the way I see it, there is not much point in having a fancy house if you never see it during the hours of daylight. I'd bet my children would rather have more father than more garden.

Stop paying so much for your front path

We pay a huge amount for the privilege of having our own car outside our house. The RAC says that motorists now spend an average of £5,539 a year paying for and running their cars – the equivalent of £15 a day or 46p a mile. On this reckoning a person on an average take-home salary works three months a year just for the car.

So I have just one question: could you find a way to do all of the things you currently do in your car without actually owning one?

I am not suggesting that you never use a car. You can if you like and many people manage fine without ever driving. I didn't get my driving license until I was 40. But cars are also genuinely useful, and many people value highly the mobility. What I am suggesting is that you could manage without *your own* car.

Now you may say that this is impossible. If you live in the country, or have throngs of small children or are elderly you may feel that a car is indispensable. OK, this section is not for you. But everywhere I go in urban areas I see perfectly able-bodied, fit, child-free people sitting in cars on their own – usually in traffic jams. It's them I want to speak to.

For those times when you love having a car – for a special journey, a holiday, for making a bunch of small trips – you hire one. Weekend hire rates start at just £12 a day. And you get to drive a brand-new car in tip-top condition. Some hire companies even deliver to your door. Alternatively, you could do a car share with friends or join one of the many new commercial car share schemes.

And once you've taken out all those really useful and fun

uses for a car, is it really worth having one at all? For much of the time a car is pure hassle. Many of us reckon that we've paid for it so we might as well use it, but more often than not we use it out of habit.

Imagine that you put the money you spend on your car into a kitty. Out of this you take the car-hire charges. You will have plenty left for paying for trains, buses and taxis whenever you need them. You can buy groceries online and have them delivered to your door for £5. You can share a friend's car to work and pay them generously. And as for all those local trips that waste so much of your time in slow traffic and hunting for a parking space, you can use a bicycle – the fastest, smartest urban people mover (see below) – or, if you are feeling lazy, buy yourself one of those fancy new electric bicycles I mentioned in on page 170 or a moped.

The real reason for letting go of a car are not to do with money, however. It is to do with stress and personal happiness. You will never again be exhausted going round and round the block hunting for a parking space or purple with rage over some petty vandalism. You will never again be stung for breakdowns, parking tickets or speeding fines. Most of the time you will be chauffeur driven, leaving you free to read, work or listen to music. You will get substantially more exercise and add years to your life. I am not claiming that public transport or cycling are stress free, but they are definitely far ahead on points.

And the only thing you will lose will be the ease of having your car at the end of your front path . So how much is that proximity costing you? If the privilege of having a personal car costs £1,000 a year more than the alternatives above then it is like papering the whole path with £20 notes. That's an awful lot of money for a small privilege.

Sexy people drive a *Veló urbaine toutes vitesse*

The bicycle offers a good example of the danger of labelling. Although it started out in the late 19th century as the must-have status symbol for rich people, by the 1930s the car was king and the bicycle was for workers getting to the foundry. Bicycles are now seen as a toy for children, an exercise machine for weekend work-outs and something that students fall off when they've drunk too much. What the bike needs is a re-branding, a new name and a sales pitch based on its unique qualities. So here goes.

Announcing Le Veló, the latest breakthrough in urban transport. Driving Le Veló you can cruise past traffic jams, drive from door to door with guaranteed parking outside and pay nothing for fuel, insurance, road tax or congestion charge. What is faster in town: a Porsche Cayenne Turbo with spoilers or a Velo X405 Mach Turbo with child seat? A few weeks ago I cycled across central London from Marble Arch to the British Museum in 12 minutes. Nothing beats that. There were two Porsches and a Mercedes convertible in the traffic jam along Wigmore Street, and I just sailed right past.

Oh, and people who ride bicycles really do get more sex. It's a fact. My mate Ashkeem cycles 16 kilometres (10 miles) to work in his tight Lycra and he gets more action than a bonobo chimpanzee, and they're not picky. He's as fit as a fiddle and ready for love.

Of course, cycling does not work for all people in all situations. They aren't great for long distances, they don't carry more than one child (although some people manage it) and they are not fun on major roads. But for the short-distance, local trips and the medium-distance trips to work, a bike has to be the best option. And yet 60 per cent of people *never* cycle 1 millimetre.

So, why don't more people cycle in town?

Is it too dangerous? The accident figures show that cycling is actually very safe. If you wear reflective clothing and don't do anything stupid you are very visible to motorists. There are plenty of designated cycle routes using side roads in most cities now.

Is it too far to cycle to work? Well this is another case of how you prioritize your living decisions. My friend Jess was looking for a new place to live, and her starting point was to look at all the good cycle routes to her office and then choose locations that fed into them. Now she cycles all along the Thames Embankment to work – surely one of the best commutes in Britain.

I think that the main reason people don't cycle is that they got out of the habit at some point in their lives and never go back to it. This is a classic case of how behaviour becomes frozen into habitual patterns.

So unfreeze the habit. Borrow a bike and try it out on side streets at quiet times of day. Notice how quick, easy and fresh it feels.

And if you really can't face pedal power, get a moped. Mopeds have many of the advantages of bicycles and have a third of the emissions of a car. That's as good as going by bus and a load sexier. So bring back *La dolce vita*.

Chapter 6

Drop a tonne on air travel
Ditching the jet set

I am a bit torn when it comes to flights. On the one hand, I'm afraid that if I tell you that you can't fly it will trigger those *don't tell me what to do – everyone else is doing it* defensive mechanisms we found among the pick-and-mix excuses for not listening (see pages 103–8).

On the other hand, I have to be honest with you. Flying is the single most destructive thing you can do. When we really deal with climate change, we will have to restrict jet travel severely. It is hard to see how we will be able to afford any flying if we cut greenhouse gas emissions by as much as we need.

If you are not much bothered by travel and fly once in a while because it is easy or cheap, then you might want to go the whole hog and decide to stop altogether. Thousands of people have already pledged to stop flying.

If you have the flying habit then don't even think of turning down your thermostat, changing your car or buying organic vegetables. Your first step towards light living has to be to fly less. Drop just one flight to a destination outside western Europe and you have dropped a tonne. And I would like you to aim to go far further than that and stop flying altogether.

As a start I suggest that you weigh up every flight on a case-by-case basis by asking:

1 Could I have an equally fun experience somewhere closer?

2 Could I travel there some other way?

3 Could I bundle up several trips so that I could go once and stay longer?

4 Can I reconfigure my life so that I do not need to make this flight?

Here is how you might answer those questions

1 Fun is far more dependent on *who* you go with than *where* you go. If it is with fun people then you could have as much fun closer to home. If it is not with fun people then why do it at all?

2 If it is a family holiday, the main thing is to keep the children happy and their needs don't require major air miles. What they want is somewhere to run around and other children. The seaside, camping and even Butlins will leave them ecstatic.

3 For trips to see family and lovers you could go less often but stay longer.

4 For the life-changing, far-away experience you could stay for a decent period of time to experience a country fully instead of whizzing in and out. Maybe you could travel all around it or do some work there.

Rather than think that you will miss great experiences or be deprived by not flying let me remind you of something. We have the huge privilege of living in the most fascinating continent in the world. We have ice and snow to the north, desert to the south, huge mountains, beaches, rivers, valleys and the richest and most diverse cultural heritage imaginable. You could spend a lifetime exploring just one corner of it – all of it is accessible by train.

I suppose at a pinch you could always have a holiday in Britain – some people even prefer it

What you must do at all costs is actively avoid any location or job decision that you know will entail major air travel. Don't even think of buying a holiday home in a place that you will have to fly to. In any case, as we saw in Part 3, buying foreign property in an unstable climate is a dangerous gamble.

And you should think very long and hard about taking a job that will involve major international travel. I know that, in theory, work travel does not count as work emissions, but there is a point at which you could also argue that, by virtue of choosing to live so far from where you need to work, the flights to get you there are a form of commuting.

A tale of two holidays

What I did during my holidays, by George Marshall, aged 42½.

Annie and I went to Italy by train. We boarded the Eurostar under the glamorous roof of Waterloo Station in central London and hurtled under the Channel and across the plains of northern France at 300 kilometres (185 miles) an hour. We arrived at the Gare du Nord in Paris and had a light lunch at a café on the square outside the station. We picked up cheese, pâté, salads, a fresh baguette and a bottle of wine from the old

---

market on the Boulevard de Magenta and caught a taxi across Paris to the Gare de Bercy taking in the Tuileries and Place de la Concorde on the way. We ate our picnic dinner on the Palatino night train and swapped our cheese with the Italian nun in our compartment for fresh salami from her family's farm. At 10 p.m. we pulled down the seats in the couchette and were gently rocked to sleep by the rhythm of the train.

The next morning we woke up early to find that everything had changed outside. Over a double espresso in the buffet car we watched the red-tiled Tuscan villages and vineyards flash by in the glorious clear Italian light. At midday we pulled into Rome Central Terminus at the very heart of the Eternal City, just in time for a plate of spaghetti at a trattoria on the Piazza de la Santa Maria Maggiore.

Or would you prefer this holiday? Alternatively, we could have sat under the lowered ceiling of a shopping mall in a field somewhere off the M25, drinking a polystyrene cup of bitter, stewed coffee. We would then have been packed into cramped seats in a hermetically sealed flying bus. We might be offered a snack of some kind – a limp sandwich filled with nameless something – on a plastic tray before being dumped at another ugly low-ceilinged shopping mall in another field 30 kilometres (20 miles) outside Rome. In between we would have seen nothing and had no more sense of travel than we would have had in a lift. Assuming that there was no engine trouble, no fog, no ice, no severe winds, no strike, no computer failure and no terrorist alert at either end, it would have been a lot quicker. Would it have been cheaper? The return train ticket from London to Rome with an overnight couchette was £130. A cheap return with Air Italia or British Airways would have been the same price. None of the tickets for those flights would have been changeable. In theory, had I been canny and booked far ahead – and been prepared to get up at dawn – I could have got a budget-airline ticket for £50 return between airports that were even harder to get to. For £80 more, we each got an extra two days and nights of holiday, a break in Paris (which could have been as long as we wanted) and the thrill of real travel.

Which holiday would you rather have?

Chapter 7

Drop a tonne on food
Eat better, live better

I promised that living light would be smarter and healthier. The way to drop a tonne on food is to stop eating processed meat products and eat a diet that is high in fresh, organic fruit and vegetables. Could there be a better prescription for a long and healthy life?

Cut back on meat

If you give up all animal products you will drop your tonne. If you are a dedicated carnivore you can still reach the target, but you will have to cut back a bit and make sure that you avoid processed food. The model low-meat option is based on the typical diet of Mediterranean countries. The main part of a meal is fresh vegetables, fruit, beans and pasta. Meat and dairy products are a small component of any meal and are often served as a separate course. This diet is strongly recommended by dieticians and has been found to prevent heart disease and, possibly, Alzheimer's disease.

Eat organic

As we have seen, you can drop a tonne straight off by eating food that has not needed artificial fertilizers. Even better, you could grow your own organic fruit and vegetables in your garden or by renting a local allotment. There are an estimated 330,000 allotments in Britain, and, after years of decline, there is a new wave of enthusiastic home growers. Once again this is a win-win for health, exercise and climate. If you combine this with eating less meat you will drop more than a tonne. If you can't face all that digging you can join an organic box scheme. Every week a local supplier delivers a box of seasonal fruit and vegetables, often less than a day out of the soil, to your doorstep.

Zero-waste home cooking

You get very near to dropping a tonne just by cooking at home using fresh seasonal ingredients. If you do this you should enforce a zero-waste policy – composting all vegetable peelings and eating every scrap of edible food. If your household is anything like ours this will mean occasional multiple-course banquets of things that have been rescued from the far corners of the fridge. In fancy restaurants they call that a 'tasting menu' and charge you double for it.

In regard to food, the carbon detox joins company with all the other detox books. In no other area are the personal benefits so clear: a diet based on seasonal, local (and ideally organic) fruit and vegetables is good for the health and good for the environment.

Chapter 8

Drop a tonne on stuff
Spend your money wisely

As someone who has been lugging junk from place to place all my life, I feel that I have no right to lecture people about stuff. At the last count Annie and I had 35 separate collections on the go, and as soon as we got rid of one (the snow domes went off to the Age Concern shop) we started another (1970s owls or recipe postcards or royal family mugs).

What I would say, though, is that our stuff is light-carbon stuff. Almost all of it was bought second-hand, and in many cases we were the last-chance saloon on its inexorable slide towards the landfill. So what can you do?

Shift your spending from things to people

As we showed in the carbo-counter on pages 222–3, the emissions of the things you buy lie along a spectrum. At one end are the manufactured goods, of which a large percentage of the cost are the energy and resources of the factory and distribution network. In the middle of the spectrum are the services. Even if they do not produce physical products they still require buildings, transport and energy. And at the far end are the labour-intensive products and services, payments to organizations and companies that are moving us towards a light-carbon world and direct gifts to other people.

To drop a tonne you will need to shift your spending sideways along that continuum from the goods to services and from general services to the high-labour products and services. Using the figures on the carbo-counter, you could drop a tonne by transferring £1,000 from heavy-carbon spending to average spending and £1,500 from average spending to light-carbon spending.

If you have enough money you can achieve the greatest carbon savings by spending money on people. You could think of them as specialist helpers with the skills to help you with certain tasks, such as childminding, cleaning or gardening. Whichever way you look at it, giving employment to local people is about the lightest carbon thing you can do.

Buy things that are made to last

Things that are well made are often those with a higher labour input. In many cases they represent a major shift on the carbo spectrum. For example, you could decide to buy a really well-made, hand-crafted chest of drawers rather than something made from chipboard and held together with staples, or you could buy a second-hand chest of drawers that will have proved its durability already.

Even if you are not moving anywhere on the spectrum, it still makes strong climate sense to pay for quality. The market for standard consumer goods is now so competitive that you really do get what you pay for. If you pay 50 per cent more you will probably get something that lasts twice as long. And being a smart, light living person, you will always pay the premium for the products with the lowest energy consumption.

Earn light

As we noticed during the carbo count, our emissions from goods and services are directly related to our disposable income. Many people have very low emissions from the things they buy because, once their basic needs are met, they have very little spare money to spend on anything. If you have a relatively high income, you will tend to have higher emissions because you have to spend your money somewhere. Even if you avoid the temptations of air travel and large houses you will still need to shift a lot of your spending into light-carbon activities in order to detox.

But there is another option. You could earn less money

I hear all of those defences clicking into place, so I will put it another way. High incomes usually come at high personal cost. They usually require all kinds of personal compromises, long hours and a lot of responsibility. After all, no one is going to pay you loads for an easy job that they could do themselves.

If you are someone who is lucky enough to be paid well for the job you love doing then I'm very happy for you. But I must say that most people I know who are earning a lot of money are being fried in the process. They assumed that they would do it for a few years and then back out. However, during those years they got locked into a heavy-carbon lifestyle complete with long-distance holidays, an expensive car and a big house – maybe even a second home. Next thing they knew they were hiring a full-time nanny to raise their children because they had to work full time to keep the whole thing afloat.

So just think about these questions. Would you like to let go of some responsibility and bring in someone else to help? Would you like to leave your current job and become a consultant – in control of your own hours and direction? Would you like to work fewer hours or have an extra day off each week? You might even find that you work so much better as a result and that you get the same amount of work done anyway. Or would you like to change to a new career and do something you feel passionate about?

All of these choices are based on the conscious decision to exchange earnings for time or satisfaction. There is now a growing movement of downscaling by people who have made these choices and are never looking back.

I write with some personal experience. Twenty years ago I pledged that I would make no compromises with my life. I have only ever done things that I felt were worthwhile and made the world better. I am no saint – this was a conscious choice and self-serving decision, which has paid dividends. I have had a truly fantastic and thrilling life and worked with the most wonderful and inspiring people you could imagine.

In 2004 I founded a climate change charity that now employs six people. I work four days a week so that I can spend one day a week with my children. When managing the organization became too stressful and started to draw me away from my pet projects (like writing this book) I hired a new executive director. I hired my own boss! Now how many people get to do that? He earns more than me, but he's the one who gets the sleepless nights.

This level of freedom is only possible because we live in a modest house, shop carefully and wisely and buy second-hand when we can. Living light is not just good for the climate – it enables us to have the freedom to do what we want to do. And that is why it is smart.

Love those wrinkles

Everything you own is second-hand, whether you like it or not. As soon as you brought something home and opened the box it lost half its value and became second-hand. It may have looked new for a while, but how long did it last? A day, a week, a month? With small children around, probably minutes. So, unless you compulsively throw out everything scuffed, I'll bet that the contents of your house looks like the contents of a charity shop, even if you paid top whack for everything.

The only real difference between buying something new and buying something second-hand is the shopping trip.

So what makes those expensive shopping trips fun? Is it the expectation of getting a treat or the ceremony of entering the shops? Are you mesmerized by the shiny surfaces and plate-glass windows – the Aladdin's cave of goodies all lined up on the shelves? Is it the kick of having what you want, when you want it?

Maybe you share the experience with a friend (real fun), partner (less fun) or family (rapidly diminishing fun). Maybe you have your own shopping rituals – a special outfit for shopping in, a coffee and cream cake afterwards? And, of course, there is that thrill of the opening up the new thing, all shiny and clean with that *new* smell. It's a fleeting thrill isn't it, like a first kiss, and one that we are always trying to recapture?

Now let me tell you why I love second-hand things. I love the thrill of hunting for something in a pile or in a box or on the rack and finding something great hiding there, just for me. I love the expectation of the car-boot sale or my regular circuit of charity shops. I love not knowing what I am going to buy until I see it.

I feel paralysed by the choice in modern stores and love having that choice made for me. I love being able to buy things on pure impulse knowing that if I don't like them, I'm only a few pence out of pocket and can sell them back into the circuit.

It is now so easy. The second-hand economy is booming. Car-boot sales sometimes have a thousand stands. Every high street has a clutch of charity shops. The Internet auction site www.ebay.co.uk is so huge that it is virtually a second-hand department store. Most areas have a 'freecycle' e-mail list on which people advertise things that they want to give away – some freecycle groups have over 10,000 members.

Hunting for second-hand things is like going to parties. Unless you are Ashkeem, the cyclist who scores every time, you usually have a fun time with your friends. Once in a while, though, you meet someone really special, and when you do it feels like they were waiting there for you to discover them.

So when I buy something second-hand, I love those wrinkles. They tell me that it has already been fully tested and will keep going. They mean that I will never be disappointed when it gets worn or old. They speak of a history with other people. Really, when you think about it, second-hand things should be *more* expensive than new things.

Chapter 9

Time to get to work
How to make these things happen

We've come a long way. We've looked at the challenges of climate change and dealt directly with the things that make it so hard for us to believe in it. We've considered your options for a personal strategy. We have examined your emissions in detail and identified the trouble areas. We've set some targets and explained some of the ways that you can reach them.

But if you really want to detox, the most challenging thing is starting the change. You are busy, the social denial is powerful and your habits run deep. Here are some suggestions for how to make it happen.

Get a carbon buddy

It is very hard to do things on your own. Even if you are completely committed to changing, there are always good reasons for putting it off. This is why it is great to have someone you know and trust who is on the journey with you. You need a buddy.

Buddies are a bit different from friends. Buddies are people who will stick with you through thick and thin. Your carbon buddy might be a partner, a close friend or a work mate. Whoever they are, they have also read this book, have made a personal commitment to live lighter and are prepared to work with you for six months.

Sit down with your buddy and arrange a programme of change and identify the things that you intend to do. If you are going to do the DIY weekend (see pages 245–8) you could pool your resources and do it together. If you are going to try something different and new you could do it with them, or one of you could try it first and report back.

Pick the dates

Throughout this section have been ideas of new things to try. But you need to give them a go or nothing will ever change in your life. With your carbon buddy, pick one or two that you have never done before and write a date on the calendar when you will do them.

What to do	When to do it
Home	
Switch to renewable energy	
Book a DIY weekend	
Call the Energy Advice Centre and book an insulation installer	
Book a home unfreezing day	
Book a day to start tweaking your energy systems	

What to do	When to do it
Food	
Cut back to meat only once a day	
Order an organic box	
Practise zero-waste home cooking	
Stuff	
Go to a car-boot sale to buy or to sell	
Buy something you want on www.ebay.co.uk	
Transport	
Ride a bike to the shops or to work	
Share your car (or someone else's car) to work	
Go on a European holiday by train	

Blue moon opportunities

Most of the time our options are limited. Things are going OK, and we really don't have the time, energy or money to change anything much.

And then suddenly we have the chance to make big changes. You've heard of blue-sky thinking. Well this is *blue moon* thinking, because these chances only come once in a blue moon and you have to grab them when they do. Although most people can fairly easily drop a first tonne or two, a large part of your long-term success in reducing your carbos will depend on your ability to spot and exploit these opportunities.

Here is an example

There is a nice, retired couple living in the last house in a Victorian terrace at the end of my road. Because their walls are solid brick and the whole flank gable wall is fully exposed to the winter winds their house is freezing in winter and they have very heavy fuel bills. Last year they paid £2,500 to renew the render on that exposed wall. For less than a £1,000 more they could have fitted solid-wall insulation behind the new render and made their house vastly warmer, healthier and cheaper for their old age. It was a blue moon opportunity that comes every 20 years and they missed it.

Any major investment in your house is an opportunity for substantially reducing its emissions at little extra cost. Building an extension or loft conversion? Pack in three times the insulation required by law. Replacing a roof? Put in a solar panel at the same time. The boiler is getting unreliable? Replace it with the most efficient boiler you can find and get thermostatic radiator valves fitted at the same time.

And then there are the even larger seismic shifts in your life – a new child, a change in your job, a new home. These are your best chances to position yourself for the changes that are coming. Make sure that among all of the many things for consideration you are also asking: will this be affected by climate change, will it reduce my emissions, will it put me in a stronger position to live light?

When you eye up that big old house ask, 'Will it be a white elephant in 20 years?' When you are tempted by the high salary of a faraway job, ask, 'Do I want to spend half my life in a traffic jam?'

If you get laid off, ask, 'Is this the opportunity to rebuild my life and do something that I am really passionate about?'

I can't answer these questions for you – but if you are asking the right questions you are halfway to finding the solutions you need for a long happy and light life. They take you to the point where you are no longer reacting to this problem but are positioned to thrive.

Part 10
Thriving

Chapter 1

Five of the best
People who really thrive

Life rewards people who are positioned for what is coming, and taking climate change seriously is like being a gambler with the inside tip.

People who have a thriving attitude decide that they are going to embrace climate change as a source of personal opportunity. They know that this issue will create the future heroes and villains, the millionaires and the bankrupts, the leaders and the losers. Although the details are still unclear, thrivers know that there is a revolution on the way and they want to be in the front line.

A thriving attitude to climate change says: 'I fully recognize the threats and dangers of climate change, but I am going to make the very best of the situation. There are lots of ways in which I can really achieve something in this new climate change world.'

But rather than hear this from me, I'd like to turn this book over to the thrivers. Here are five of my favourite people – people who have heard the historic calling of climate change and have turned their lives around. Not one of them is a scientist or expert or career environmentalist. All of them took substantial personal risks in order to engage with an issue that was new and marginal at the time.

And now all of them are thriving. They love their work and their lives. They have found direction, success and boundless new opportunities. Although they are well aware of the scale and seriousness of the issue, their attitude is overwhelmingly positive because all they can see are solutions.

Penney Poyzer

Penney's extraordinary career has been built out of her personal mission: to communicate to people the benefits of light-carbon living. She has worked in many fields in her life – journalism, public relations, community development, local government. She describes her career as 'one long training programme', where each job has given her new insights and skills for the next. She is very conscious of 'living in the now', always moving on to new projects and finding new ways to communicate better with people.

In 1998 she moved with her partner Gill into a large Victorian house in Nottingham and set out to show how much could be achieved with an old and inefficient house. They put everything they could afford into it. They insulated the walls, put solar panels on the roof, collected rain water and sewage in the cellar and installed a wood boiler powered by waste pallets.

But Penney didn't want to stop there. She wanted to tell everyone about it, so she set up a website about the house and gave guided tours to the public. She reckons that nearly a thousand people have visited. One time, an entire Parliamentary Select Committee set up hearings in her living room. Penney says it was the first time that any Parliamentary committee has held an official sitting in a private house.

She started appearing in newspapers and on the TV and radio. After one item on BBC Radio Four's *Woman's Hour* she received a phone call from a television company inviting her to present a new television series. When *No Waste Like Home* went out on BBC2 in 2005 it was watched by around 2 million people a week. Penney wrote a book about the series and now has two more in the pipeline. Her life is now a constant whirlwind of activity, speaking engagements and new projects.

She says: 'My life is amazing. I feel blessed to know exactly what my purpose is in life. I don't have to waste any time prevaricating over my career choices or resenting my job or hating the office politics. I love to be independent, working alongside people but not to be owned by anyone. I have been given this fantastic opportunity to do something driven and to say we *can* make a change.'

Mike Lawton

While Mike was an engineering student he was intrigued to read that Rudolf Diesel had originally invented the diesel engine to run on vegetable oil. He tinkered with his own beaten-up old car and ran it for the next two years on waste oil from the local chip shop.

For the next few years he worked as an electrical engineer, developing power systems for satellites. He did not lose his fascination for vegetable fuels, however, and with the growing awareness and concern about climate change, he saw a great business opportunity. With a partner, he set up a company to develop a controller that can convert any diesel engine to run on low-grade vegetable oil.

Although his technology can be used on any diesel engine, Mike is fascinated by the idea of making the largest and heaviest vehicles carbon neutral. His system has been used to convert buses and large trucks as far afield as Turkey and Singapore. In 2007 he enjoyed a world first – a deep-sea trawler running entirely on vegetable fuel.

Mike shared the concerns of many environmentalists that using vegetable oils in engines would waste agricultural land and lead countries to cut down rainforest. He is now looking at ways to exploit poor-quality, non-edible vegetable oils, especially those from an Asian plant called jatropha. It is, he says, a weed species that grows in desolate areas that are too poor for crops. He is looking to develop jatropha as a Fair Trade fuel oil that can return income to the poorest parts of India.

Mike's company, Renenetec, has doubled in size each year. He was amazed by the interest in his products. 'We've never placed a single advert,' he says. 'All we did was respond to market interest. When we started, I assumed that businesses would only be interested if I talked about how much money they can save, but we are finding that many companies are interested simply because we can reduce their fleet emissions.'

Mike says: 'I love showing doubters that the technology works. I derive immense satisfaction from knowing that all I need to do is to get one major company to shift to this technology and I will have saved far more emissions than I could ever save in my own life. I don't think I could ever go back to a standard job. Working for a large company is like being on a cruise liner and this is more like white-water rafting! Tony Blair came to visit our offices. We gave him a ride and I got 20 minutes sitting in my office chatting to the prime minister about renewable energy. Now what normal job gives you that?!'

Pauline Lazoya

As soon as Pauline speaks – and she speaks very fast indeed – she bubbles with energy and enthusiasm for her work. 'This is the big issue,' she says, 'and if you can communicate it right you can see the climate change penny drop for anyone.'

Pauline would never fit the stereotype of a 'green campaigner'. She grew up in a working-class Manchester family and has spent most of her working life as a teacher in some of Britain's toughest schools. In 2001 she was teaching Spanish and French in Wythenshawe – at that time the most deprived ward in the European Union – when she started to talk about climate change with her pupils. She said, 'I started to feel really angry about it because I felt that their rights to a future were being taken away from them.' The teenagers felt the same way, and they formed an action group inside the school called Rite2no.

The project grew in scale and ambition. The Rite2no group held special assemblies and, with Pauline's help, travelled all round Britain, interviewing scientists and politicians about the problem. The group started making a video about climate change and held a festival in a local park.

In 2006 Rite2no won a government grant to expand the project and distribute the video. At this point Pauline decided to throw herself fully into the project.

'I've made a huge leap of faith – to jump out of job security and into, well, who knows what? But it feels great. I'm happier right now that I've been at any time in my life – definitely. I feel that my life has a real meaning and I am working on what is really important. Anyway, the changes that are coming are so huge that all of that traditional career planning is up in the air. This is what is important right now.'

Paul Bodenham

Paul Bodenham felt his first real foreboding about climate change on the eve of the new millennium. He remembers vividly a news report from the first country to witness the New Year from the Pacific islands of Kiribati. The reporter said, almost as an aside that, because of sea level rise, the islands would no longer be there in fifty years. 'This really struck home,' he says. 'It made me feel that there were two worlds – the one in which we were all supposed to be celebrating the next thousand years and the one in which there was this unrecognized crisis that no one was talking about.' In October that year he was woken up by a huge crash as a 145-kph (90-mph) wind blew a slate off his roof. He decided it was time to do something.

Paul was no campaigner – his background was as an officer for local government and the Countryside Agency – but he was a highly committed Christian and believed he had a moral responsibility to do something. He was shocked to find that the Church had no position, no policy and was saying nothing at all about this huge problem. He decided to change that.

Operating from his front room, he launched Operation Noah as a call to Christians to take action on climate change. It moved slowly at first because Paul had virtually no funding and had to fit the campaign around his normal work. He started with a simple 'covenant' on which people pledged to reduce their emissions. As the project grew, 3,000 people signed the covenant.

In 2004 Operation Noah was officially launched by the Bishop of Hereford at a special service at Coventry Cathedral. Hundreds of churches followed by holding services dedicated to climate change – with hymns, sermons and readings that celebrated God's creation and recognizing the challenge of the new threat. By 2007 Operation Noah had funded staff and the full backing of Churches Together, the ecumenical body that brings together all 40 mainstream Christian denominations.

Paul says: 'I knew all along that this would be a lot of work. I thought I must be mad. But I never thought twice about doing it. This work has completely changed the way that I see the world and made me into a much more aware person. What always amazes me is that, now, I don't feel too bothered about climate change itself. Somehow, when you feel that you are reaching people and feel that you are being effective you really do feel that you have power.'

Antony Turner

Antony Turner's personal journey started in the most unlikely place: supporting the North Sea oil industry. His first job was working for the largest supplier of steel for the oil platforms, and he went on to a very successful business career developing technology for the underwater electrical connectors used in the pipelines.

But as he reached 40, he started having major misgivings about the direction his life had taken. He decided to take time out to re-evaluate what he was doing and achieving. At about this time he started to become aware of the scale and threat of climate change. He knew the business world very well and was convinced that it could be a powerful force for good, but he was deeply concerned that it was not being communicated in a way that business people could understand or appreciate. He decided to take up the challenge.

In 2003 Antony went back into business in a quite new way: his new company, called Carbonsense, would engage businesses about climate change. He developed a creative multimedia presentation called a 'carbon journey', during which managers were helped to become 'carbon positive' and look at climate change as a business opportunity. With funding from the Carbon Trust, Antony made presentations to many major companies and government departments, including the Treasury.

In 2005 Carbonsense had a major break: British Telecom commissioned the company to lead an internal visioning exercise entitled 'What would a carbon-neutral BT look like?' Carbonsense told BT management to imagine themselves in the future, assessing their successful leadership on climate change. It seems to have worked. BT has just appointed an internal 'head of climate change' and is determined to be a leader among the telecommunications companies.

Carbonsense now has seven staff members and is expanding exponentially with several major contracts under negotiation. Antony is hugely excited about his new direction in life and the work he is doing. 'It is great to be doing work that I feel is good,' he says. 'It feels both fantastic and knackering! If I was not doing this work I could get very depressed about climate change. But I derive enormous hope from finding that if you touch powerful people in the right way, amazing things can happen.'

Just think for a moment of what Antony said there: by accepting climate change and focusing his skills on it he is able to feel excited and positive about a huge and frightening problem. All my thrivers reported the same thing. Action really is the antidote to despair.

Part 11
Taking control

Chapter 1

Closing down the rollercoaster

Reasons for taking control

Every action you take creates ripples of change. Everything you say and do about climate change rubs off on the people around you and makes it more relevant in their own lives. And every time you decide to do something positive, you synchronize the dance between your beliefs and your actions and you reinforce the story you tell yourself about who you are and what is important to you.

And every time you decide to do something positive, you synchronize the dance between your beliefs and your actions and you reinforce the story you tell yourself about who you are and what is important to you.

Personal action is meaningful, even if no one ever hears about it. However, if this is all you do I think that you may well be missing a trick

For one thing, if you really believe in the scale and immediacy of this threat, then you know we can't afford just to wait for lots of little ripples to join up. Surely you have some responsibility to go beyond your immediate interests and actively engage others. If you do nothing more than tell people what you have done you will still have greatly increased your influence.

Second, you still have the problem of that Evil Carbon Twin hanging around. Even if you are modest and self-effacing, your carbon twin is not. He is bragging about his big new car and his holiday in Florida. My observation is that the more pointless and empty are the things that people do, the harder they work to seek outside validation for them. It is as though they know the truth but think they can lobby people to persuade them otherwise.

And third, we have to recognize that those people who say 'the government will have to sort it out' and 'I'll do it until they make it illegal' do have a point. We are never really going to deal with this until the government changes the rules of the game and starts shifting those sticks and carrots. And that change is not going to happen unless we *demand* it.

For all of these reasons the final strategy for dealing with climate change is called taking control

Taking control is the stage in your personal journey when, having accepted climate change and built it into your own life planning, you decide that you want to generate wider change.

Taking control is not for everyone. You may wish just to

adapt or live lighter and leave it there for the moment. Even if you want to thrive, you may wish to limit yourself to making climate change related career choices.

This is the slimmest part of the book for a good reason: taking control is not a programme with readily identifiable steps. It is an *attitude*, and how you choose to take control is entirely a matter of your own inclination and opportunity. Speaking to your neighbours, writing to a newspaper, mobilizing a community group, lobbying an MP or holding a protest are all very different activities and appeal to very different people with different approaches to the world. The only thing they have in common is a desire to effect wider change.

In the following chapters I outline three ways you might think about taking control: Amplify, Multiply and Rectify. But in case you are worried that this sounds like the chant for some cult, I repeat – this section is very much about giving you some ideas. There is no carbon bottom line in this section, and what you choose to do and how you choose do it are very much up to you.

Chapter 2

Amplify

Why it is good to talk about yourself

You understand climate change and are
living light. You want to tell people all about
the problem, why it is so important and
what you have done about it.

This is a crucial component of social change. As we now
know, people take their cues for what is important from the
people around them. When you amplify you are
establishing that climate change is important and has a
relevance to other people's lives.

However, as I have warned, you may find that people are
not willing to engage with this issue. They have their own
pick-and-mix excuses, their own obstacles to believing and
a set of ready-made labels to attach to people who challenge
them – eco-freaks, communists, spoilsports, killjoys, doom-
mongers. Remember that this is nothing to do with you.
These defence strategies are all based on fear: a fear of the
issue, a fear of change and a fear of being judged.

When you hear people talk about climate change on the
television they invariably use language that triggers all of
these defense mechanisms. For example, they might say,
'Scientists tell us that the planet weather systems are
changing because of the way that we live. This is the biggest

problem ever faced by humanity and it will be even worse for our children. We need to take immediate action to change our lifestyles because soon it will be too late.'

The speaker is trying to make it sound authoritative and inclusive but achieves the opposite. What people actually hear is: 'Someone who doesn't know about this himself is telling me that someone else says that I am responsible for landing my children (whom I love) in a horrible mess and that it is up to me to give something up.' Is it any surprise that people feel judged and don't want to accept it?

So here is the golden rule for amplifying climate change: **talk about yourself**. Talk about what *you* believe, what *you* feel, what *you* can see and what *you* are doing about it. No one can disagree with what you believe, even if they don't agree with your reasons for believing it

For example, imagine how much more effective it would be to hear someone say: 'I am very concerned about climate change. I trust what the scientists are saying and it sounds very serious. And I can see the changes myself. This year all the daffodils in my garden came up in December – now I find that really worrying. So I decided that I would look at my own contribution to this problem and my first resolution was never to fly on holiday any more. This year I went by train to Cornwall and had a great time – I really recommend it.'

Doesn't that make you want to know more?

When you live light, you make numerous changes that are of direct interest and relevance to people around you. You could tell people about how much warmer your house is since you got your cavities insulated, how much cheaper your new car is to run, how great it is to be working closer to home, how great it is to cycle to the shops. And when you mention climate change you are not lecturing them, but simply providing an additional context for your actions. Remember, you've got that insider tip so you are just a little ahead of the pack. When they get it too, they will recognize and respect the fact that you were there first.

If you do phrase it in this unthreatening way, you will be surprised by how receptive people are. I would never recommend anything that I hadn't tried myself. I have tried this non-threatening approach many, many times in the course of casual conversations – with people in the queue at the bus stop, the mechanic at the garage, my neighbours, another parent at the family centre. Most times it is just an aside, but occasionally it really plants a seed. All I can say is: it works.

And if you are feeling bold there is no limit to how many people you can tell. As this issue heats up, every newsletter, magazine, newspaper, radio and TV channel in Britain is looking for real stories about the things that people are doing to prevent climate change. Through them you can reach and inspire many more people. Just think about how thriver Penney Poyzer started out by doing what she believed in and has ended up reaching millions of people (see pages 285–6).

So why not write an article for a local magazine or contact your local newspaper and radio station and offer to give them an interview? Why not start a website or write a blog? It has to be worth a try.

Chapter 3
Multiply
Helping people take their own action

Amplifying is being open and upfront about what you are doing and what you believe in. Multiplying is going a stage further and actively seeking to help people to take action for themselves. Mutiplying is about converting the Evil Carbon Twins to Carbon Angels.

If you are a multiplier you are thinking of all the places where you might have some influence. Obviously you can help and advise anyone in your personal circle. If you have a carbon buddy you will already be working with him or her, and you could invite other people you know to team up with you and join in your project to drop a tonne.

But it doesn't have to stop there. Are you member of a society, a community organization, a trade union, a political party, a church? All of them need to be thinking about climate change and are waiting for someone to break the ice, so to speak. Raise it at a meeting and suggest that there could be an open discussion about the issue and what, collectively, you could do about it.

Alternatively, you could form a group. During the past

year I have been thrilled to see hundreds of new community organizations forming around climate change. They all started with a few people who came together and decided to do something. Most of them are looking in detail at the lifestyles of the people in the group, but a few have turned into something far more ambitious and are trying to reduce emissions for their entire community.

And then there is work. So far this book has been concerned with personal action and has deliberately excluded your work emissions. After all, most people work in large companies and organizations where they get little say over their small corner.

So just ask yourself these questions: Where might I have some influence over emissions from my work?. Can I see an opportunity to reduce energy use or transport? Is there a decision-making process within which I could suggest a climate change policy? Does my employer have an existing commitment to reducing emissions that could be upheld, enforced or strengthened?

Chapter 4

Rectify

Using your power

As you grappled with reducing your emissions you will certainly have felt on occasion that the whole world is against you. You can't find the information you need or the product you want is out of stock or is too expensive or no one knows how to install it or the bus is late or the train is fully booked.

And there are more fundamental structural problems. You would prefer to take the bus to work, but it runs only once an hour. You would like to make local trips by bicycle, but it just feels too dangerous on your local roads.

And then there are the times when your desire to live differently comes up against other people's heavy-carbon standards. Your partner insists on a Mediterranean beach holiday. Your sister wants everyone to fly to her dream wedding in the Bahamas.

In each of these cases you encounter the same problem – society is fundamentally geared to heavy-carbon living. Politicians and business leaders talk all the time about the *need* for change but seem unwilling or unable to break free of the heavy-carbon economic model.

Rectifying is the decision to challenge this inertia and demand change. Of all the strategies, this is the most overtly political because the government is such a key player in setting national policy. Progressive government policy can encourage public transport, provide affordable homes close to work, discourage flying and make solar power cheap and accessible. And, at present, the government is still a major supporter of destructive development: of airport expansion, road building and oil development.

Local government also has a great deal of influence for good and for bad. The planning decisions made by local authorities decide where people will live, work and shop for generations. Local authorities routinely nod through new developments that will lock thousands of people into car dependency.

You may choose work within the system and fully utilize the existing channels for dissent.

As a customer or a shareholder you have a say in how businesses are run. As a member of the public you have a legally enshrined right to complain about any advertisement, article or programme that you believe is inaccurate or misleading. As a television viewer you have a right to complain about coverage that misrepresents the issues. As a voter you have every right to make it clear to your MP or councillor that your vote is dependent on their position on climate change.

Or you may choose to go in a quite different direction – organizing vocal and visible protests, creating your own media and messages or supporting and inspiring an opposi- tional movement for change. No major social change has ever come without a combination of different strategies – cautious and radical, inside and outside, practical and visionary, reformist and revolutionary – and we need to respect and nurture all approaches. I could tell you about hundreds of exciting initiatives that need your enthusiasm and support.

But I'm not going to. As you know, this book is about encouraging you to *believe* that you can do something rather than telling you what you can do. Like all the other aspects of taking control, rectification is an *attitude* that you bring to your engagement with climate change. Once you have that attitude and decide that you want to do something there is no shortage of things that you can do – they are everywhere. And there can be no stopping you.

Part 12
Living the detox

Chapter 1

Living the detox

How it feels to live in balance with the climate

So far I have spoken of other people and their experiences. It's time for me to come out from behind the curtain and talk about my own experience of the detox.

I will be honest with you – living light is not the easiest option. For the past seven years I have been steadily doing all the things in this book. Sometimes it has been deeply rewarding and sometimes, to tell you the truth, it has been a right pain.

Nonetheless, I am absolutely convinced that this is not just a better and smarter life but the *only* option for the future. The frustrations come from being a pioneer and waiting for the rest of the world to catch up.

Like Paul Bodenham, whom we met with the Thrivers, my journey started on the eve of the millennium as I looked into the future and considered my place in it. I had been working abroad for several years on rainforest conservation but had become frustrated and disenchanted. When my contract ended I made no attempt to extend it and moved back to Britain with my new wife, Annie.

There I was in a cold bleak British December with no job, no plans and the rest of my life in front of me. It was one of those rare 'blue moon' opportunities that it is so important to recognize and exploit. It was a chance to stop, think and change. An easy option would have been to start looking for a new job, hopefully with decent money, that drew on my existing experience and skills. Instead, I made a wild jump into the unknown and decided that I would dedicate the rest of my life to stopping climate change.

I had never made any form of life pledge like this before and I feared that it might be too self-limiting and a shade pretentious, but I had become convinced of the importance of climate change and knew that there was plenty to do. My instincts were right. Deciding to work on just this one thing has been liberating because it has provided a structure and theme to my life. New opportunities are opening up all the time, and I cannot imagine that I will ever feel bored in this work. Above all, I can afford to experiment because nothing I do can ever be a mistake. Even if something doesn't work I still gain new contacts, ideas and experience that I can carry through to my next project.

But I'm jumping ahead. Back in 2000 I had three things in my life: my mum, my lovely wife Annie, with whom I was intending to start a family, and a terraced house on an Oxford council estate that I had bought because it seemed cheap and a good place to put my savings. The first step in my new life was to sort out this house.

It was a pretty horrible house that had suffered a disastrous bout of incompetent DIY followed by years of of eclectic interior decoration in the hands of hippy tenants. There was mildew all around the bathroom, drooping pink pine panelling in the kitchen, a bright yellow living room festooned with spangly stars, third-rate aluminium windows and 'Cotswold-style' stone cladding on the front wall that, thankfully, fell off with a huge crash in the middle of the night.

The house was a blue moon opportunity, and we duly ripped the thing apart. We covered the scars left by the stone cladding with thick external insulation, replaced the kitchen with recycled oak furniture, built a new extension with a turf roof and three times more insulation than required by law. We bought low-energy appliances and put solar panels on the roof. We had a great builder and a dreadful building inspector, who held up work for weeks at a time. As I said, it is not easy being a pioneer. But the end result was worth it. Our home is bright and fresh. It is warm in winter and very cool in summer. And, because the renovation needed doing anyway, it cost only a few thousand pounds more to do it to these far higher specifications.

Our house now uses one-third of the gas, electricity and water of the houses on either side. I know because I take their metre readings for comparison. The UK government wants to reduce house emissions by 60 per cent by 2050, and I exceeded this level in just two years. When we finally get serious about climate change every old house in Britain will have to be rebuilt this way.

It seemed to me, though, that there was little point in doing all this unless I told other people about it. As I urge in this book, I decided to amplify and multiply. I started showing people around the house – friends, students, councillors and even the senior management team from the Oxford City Council housing department. I heard that the Lotteries Commission was giving small grants for community projects, and I obtained enough money to hire a website designer. Six years later the site, www.theyellowhouse.org.uk, has been visited by over 600,000 people and I still receive a letter a week from someone saying that they they have been inspired to do something themselves.

Annie and I do all of the things recommended in this book. Our vegetables come from a local organic box scheme. Annie keeps my carnivorism in check and pork pies (made from local free-range pigs) have become more of a dietary supplement than a staple. The vast majority of our clothes, toys, furniture and tableware is second-hand. We treat car-boot sales and charity shops as a kind of hire service – we buy things and, when we've used them, we return them to the source. We are not puritans: we like to own nice things and still buy new when we fancy something special, but we see no reason to waste money on junk.

For a long time we managed without a car. I had survived 40 years quite happily without a driving license and found a bike and public transport perfectly manageable, even with one child. But when child number two came along we reluctantly bit the bullet and joined the car owning-society.*

I expected that when I finally had a car I would suddenly understand what everyone was on about – that I would discover this fantastic 'freedom' that the ads promised and understand why my friends have been pouring thousands of pounds a year into their personal motors. And I do see the point when I am out early in the morning on the open road, or exploring some out-of-the-way village. But I am also astonished to discover that most of the time driving a car in town is utter pants – tedious, time consuming and exasperating. So even though I have a car it rarely gets used more than once a week for local trips and maybe once a month for a longer trip or a visit to my mum. It has hardly transformed my life.

*We would gladly use hire cars but we need a car close to hand because my son has been prone to asthma attacks and needs a night-time run to the hospital. Sadly, there is no viable car share in our neighbourhood, although I try to lend my car to people as often as I can.

Doing without flying has been a lot harder. Annie is American, and her family and friends are a long way away. But she is determined not to fly and the last time we went was three years ago for her mother's funeral. We don't know when we might go again, but if we do we will stay a good while and maybe rent a place to live for a while.

In a way it is harder for me than Annie because I suffer badly from wanderlust: it would have been me begging to be Captain Cook's cabin boy. I get my travel urge fuelled by train travel and staying closer to home. I don't totally rule out a long-haul flight some time in the future, but if I do it will be for a long, long stay.

And finally, my work. In 2000 I knew virtually nothing about climate change beyond the articles I read in the newspapers. I wasn't sure how to start, but I thought I would just get going and see where it took me. After seven years I am still constantly thrilled by the new opportunities that open up all the time to work in new areas and learn new skills. I have no training in journalism, but I have been invited to write articles for the *New Statesman*, the *Ecologist* and the *Guardian*. I have no training in film-making, but I have made three films and contributed to numerous documentaries. I have no specific qualifications in business, environment or architecture yet I have worked as a consultant to major national companies and regularly speak at conferences about good business practice and low-energy design.

I have spoken about climate change all over the country – once I travelled across the country to a public meeting where only two people turned up, one of whom wanted to 'solve' climate change by flashing his naked bottom at heads of state. Another time I addressed over a thousand people in Central Hall, Westminster – that was terrifying.

In 2000 I was one of a handful of people who set up an international grassroots campaign network called Rising Tide. In the UK we ran three national roadshows and organized a spate of non-violent direct action protests. When we started there were virtually no climate change protests. Now there are marches and protests involving thousands of people.

In 2004 I decided I wanted to work in a different way. I founded a new charity, the Climate Outreach Information Network (COIN), and built it up to a full-time staff of six people. My current work with COIN includes designing a national adult educational curriculum for Ruskin College and developing the first interactive website for home renovators. Needless to say, I have never previously worked on educational curricula or website design.

All of this underlines what we heard earlier from the Thrivers – if you throw yourself into this work you can find endless opportunities to do new things, work in new areas and meet quite wonderful and inspiring new people. My work is constantly challenging and thrilling. Like the other Thrivers, I feel much better about climate change knowing that I am making real progress. I don't know what will happen in the future, but I am damned well not going to go down without a fight.

In December 2006 Gaia approached me to write a book that could appeal to a new audience, telling them about climate change and helping them reduce their own climate impacts. And guess what? I had never written a book before. But what the hell, I thought, let's give it a go!

You are now finishing that book, and I hope that you enjoyed it. Please feel inspired to do something yourself, starting today.

Chapter 2

Your next steps
How to get started

This book was written to make the detox
sound as easy and possible. The real
challenge, though, is actually starting the
process and, as I have said, there are
plenty of obstacles, real and imagined.
So I will keep it very simple:

Visit www.carbondetox.org

I have worked with my colleagues in the Climate Outreach
Information Network (COIN) to set up a website to help
steer you in the right direction. We will ask you a few
questions about who you are and where you want to go and
give you a small number of well-chosen contacts that can
help you on the journey.

We know that it can feel lonely up there on the rollercoaster, and we know that trying to live differently can
sometimes feel like you are swimming upstream. So we will
do everything we can to link you up with other people who
can share their own fears, hopes and frustrations and help
you realize that you are not on your own but are at the front
of a wave of change.

We would also love to hear from you at COIN. Our small
team runs an ambitious programme of training events,

workshops, public meetings and practical information-sharing projects. We are the only charity with the core mission of engaging the public about climate change, and we would love to have your support or involvement.

You can find out more about us as www.coinet.org.uk, or you can contact info@coinet.org .uk or call 01865 727 911.

Finally, if you are interested in the issues we addressed in Part 4: Overcoming denial and truly believing in climate change, you might like to visit my blog, www.climatedenial.org, where I post stories on our confused and evasive response to climate change. It is lively and chatty and has guest postings by some of the top names in environmental journalism. Please do join in the intense debates that rage in the forum section.

Appendices

Further reading

There are many books available on climate change and lifestyle. I was tempted to review them all but I really don't want to have some nasty confrontation with an offended author. So here is a personal selection of my favourites – and there are new ones coming out all the time.

The climate rollercoaster

The Rough Guide to Climate Change by Robert Henson (Rough Guides) is the best written and most accessible all-round briefing. It's also fun to see how a travel guide book company gets caught up in knots justifying its core business in the face of climate change, but at least they aren't ignoring it.

For a summary of the science I recommend *Global Warming: The Complete Briefing* by John Houghton (Cambridge University Press). It is technical but understandable to a layperson. You can also go to the source and try reading the Assessment Reports of the Intergovernmental Panel on Climate Change (www.ipcc.ch/pub/reports.htm). I warn you, though, that they are extremely turgid.

For an overview of the impacts I strongly recommend *Six Degrees: Our Future on a Hotter Planet* by Mark Lynas (Fourth Estate). Mark is probably the first journalist to systematically read and compile research from across all the science disciplines. Fred Pearce, a highly regarded *New Scientist* regular, explores the same topic in *The Last Generation: How Nature Will Take Her Revenge for Climate Change* (Eden Books), which, as its title suggests, is a cheery read.

The vision

I recommend two excellent books on solutions.

Heat: How We Can Stop the Planet Burning by George Monbiot (Penguin) is immensely readable and provides a daunting but possible scenario for a 90 per cent cut in UK emissions.

My second choice deserves to be much better known. *Stormy Weather: 101 Solutions to Global Climate Change* by Guy Dauncey and Patrick Mazza (New Society) provides practical solutions for every possible audience – individuals, groups, businesses, national and international governments. It is impossible not to read this book and feel enthused by the possibility of these changes.

Carbon counting and low-carbon living

There is now a good range of general lifestyle books on the market. Here are my favourites.

All the talk about 'ethical' living in *A Good Life: The Guide to Ethical Living* by Leo Hickman (Eden Books) might not go down well with Winner types, but this is a very thorough and beautifully presented book.

Save Cash and Save the Planet by Andrea Smith and Nicola Baird (Collins) is written by a team at Friends of the Earth, and, as the title suggests, it is rather geared toward Strivers. It is attractive enough to eat and written in an easy, popular style. I especially like the way that it incorporates ideas and comments from 'ordinary' people.

I also recommend *How to Live the Low-carbon Life: The Individual's Guide to Stopping Climate Change* by Chris Goodall (Earthscan Publications). No other book packs more information to the pound. If there is such a thing as a carbon nerd, Chris Goodall would fit the bill – the *Financial Times* calls him its 'low-carbon 'guru'. This is certainly the most detailed analysis available and the best book for the hard-core detoxer.

The title *How We can Save the Planet* by Mayer Hillman and Tina Fawcett (Penguin) is misleading. Although this book contains a good carbon counter, it is actually a persuasive manifesto for personal carbon rationing. It has inspired a growing number of carbon rationing groups and started a very important debate.

As handy tips book go, *Saving the Planet without Costing the Earth: 500 Simple Steps to a Greener Lifestyle* by Donnachadh McCarthy (Fusion Press) is the best. Donnachadh writes a lifestyle column for the *Independent* and really knows his stuff. Certainly it gave me some new ideas.

Drop a tonne

There are too many specialist books and information sources on energy and emissions reduction to profile all of them here. I will limit myself to just two favourites:

For those wishing to drop a tonne at home and especially the DIY weekenders I strongly recommend *The Eco-house Manual: How to Carry Out Environmentally Friendly Improvements to Your Home* by Nigel Griffiths (Haynes). The Haynes Guide style will be familiar to all home car mechanics – simple, well illustrated and relevant.

For those wishing to drop a tonne on food, I really like *21st-Century Smallholder: From Window Boxes To Allotments – How To Go Back To The Land Without Leaving Home* by Paul Waddington (Eden Books). It is not great as a how-to book but it is fun, engaging and inspiring, which is a pretty good start.

I have written more books on the book website: www.carbondetox.org.

References, explanations and interesting thoughts

Part 1: Fresh ways to think about climate change

Oh, not another bloody polar bear!

Many people have pointed out that it is strange that, at the very time that polar bears and penguins are most at risk from climate change, they are appearing with such regularity in popular entertainment. For an interesting take on this see www.climatedenial.org/2006/12/08/moviegoers-poles-apart-on-climate-change/

The only thing that counts is the carbon bottom line

This is how Craig Simmons did his calculations. An unpublished draft paper by Nick Brooks and W. Neil Adger from the Tyndall Centre for Climate Change Research, 'Country Level Risk Indicators from Outcome Data on Climate-related Disasters', suggests that 250 million more people are now being killed and severely affected each year by climate-related disasters than before the 1970s. Even though only half of current emissions are forcing climate change, they will, according to Intergovernmental Panel on Climate Change (IPCC) estimates, lead to a doubling in the number of people affected by climate change. So Craig felt justified in taking this figure as an estimate of the people affected by climate change and dividing it by current emissions.

As Craig points out, there are many weaknesses with the raw data and many non-climate variables on the numbers of people affected by any individual disaster, including wealth, health, the level of preparedness and the effectiveness of the government response. So, as I say, these figures must be seen as very rough indeed.

The death of a thousand tips

The Institute of Public Policy Research (IPPR) report I quote here is 'Warm Words: How are we Telling the Climate Story and can we Tell it Better?' It is downloadable at www.ippr. org.

Part 2: Make this book work for you

In addition to the reports listed in Part 7: Preparing for the detox, I drew strongly on a series of articles by Chris Rose, former campaigns director for Greenpeace UK. Chris has argued very persuasively that environmentalists tend to assume that everyone is like them and fail to recognize the wide range in actual public attitudes. Drawing on a marketing methodology developed by Pat Dade of Cultural Dynamics, Chris divides the population into pioneer, prospector and settler groups. These approximate to my Striver, Winner and Survivor groups. Of the papers posted in the resources section of his website, www.campaignstrategy.org, I recommend *A Tool for Motivation Based Communication Strategy* as a good starting point on his thinking.

Part 3: The climate rollercoaster

Although the rollercoaster analogy is my own, there are many people trying to find a new language to explain climate change as an experience and journey. One of my inspirations in this regard has been Joanna Macey, whose essay 'Facing Climate Change and Other Great Adventures' can be found at www.coinet.org.uk/information/perspectives.

The rollercoaster site where I found the most obsessive 'coastie' talk about g-forces and whipping curves was www.ultimaterollercoaster.com. Albert Einstein enthuses about them in *The Evolution of Physics*.

Up the lift hill

To estimate the atom bomb equivalent I took the IPCC calculation that the energy enhancement of the total greenhouse effect is 1,200,000 gigawatts, of which two-thirds is due to the human increase in greenhouse gases. I then divided this by the energy released by the Hiroshima atom bomb (estimated at 2.8×10^{12} joules).

Working from different figures, D. Wilks reaches the conclusion that the total additional energy from the enhanced greenhouse effect is nearly five Hiroshima bombs per second. See www.interflush.co.uk/htm/GlobalWarmingmeasuredinhiroshimabombs.doc.

Either way, it's a lot of energy.

You're already on the rollercoaster

The stories about the winter of 2006–2007 were taken from the mainstream newswire services – mostly Reuters. The *New York Times* did a full story about the Austrian downhill ski championships on 19 January 2007 in which the president of the International Ski Federation, Gian Franco Kasper, stated categorically, and in defiance of scientific opinion, that the chronic lack of snow was down to natural variation. Clearly this is a man in denial.

Over the top

Most of the material about Britain comes from the national and regional reports on the website of the UK Climate Impacts Programme. They have prepared a map of the impacts of different sea level rises at www.ukcip. org.uk/news_releases/44.gif. Estimates of UK flooding impacts come from the Foresight report I cite in Part 5.

For the international impacts, the main source is the Fourth Assessment Report of the Intergovernmental Panel on Climate Change, which can be downloaded at www.ipcc.ch/SPM6avr07.pdf.

The Potsdam paper is at www.pikpotsdam.de/~anders/ publications/sea-level.pdf.

The World Bank paper is at www.wds.worldbank.org/ external/default/WDSContentServer/IW3P/IB/2007/02/ 09/000016406_20070209161430/Rendered/PDF/ wps4136.pdf (I bet you wished you hadn't asked).

James Hanson's arguments that the sea level rise will be far higher than predicted can be found at http://pubs. giss.nasa.gov/docs/2007/2007_Hansen_etal_2.pdf. The *Guardian* journalist George Monbiot said of this report: 'Reading a scientific paper on the train this weekend, I found, to my amazement, that my hands were shaking. This has never happened to me before, but nor have I ever read anything like it.'

You can see dynamic maps of the impacts of different global sea level rises at www.geo.arizona.edu/dgesl/ research/other/climate_change_and_sea_level/sea_ level_rise/sea_level_rise.htm.

The full World Health Organization report on climate

change and health is at www.who.int/globalchange/climate/summary/en/index.html.

The 2004 report on mass extinctions from nature is at www.mindfully.org/Air/2004/Extinction-Climate-Change8jan04.htm.

The Hadley Centre report on the die-back of the Amazon rainforest can be found at www.metoffice.gov.uk/research/hadleycentre/pubs/HCTN/HCTN_42.pdf.

Part 4: Overcoming denial and truly believing in climate change

The background to this section can be found in *Painting the Town Green*, a report by the Green Engage project that summarizes all the main academic research on green communications and interviews many of the key people in the green movement. See www.green-engage.co.uk/project_painting.html.

A good short introduction to the issue of public communication by Simon Retallack of the IPPR can be found at http://www.truthout.org/issues_06/051906EA.shtml. There are papers on the same topic by myself and George Monbiot at www.coinet.org.uk/information/perspectives.

Be unnatural

The concept of a 'risk thermostat' comes from the work of Professor John Adams and is discussed in his book *Risk* (Routledge).

A curious aside about our psychological need for an enemy. If you go onto the Internet and search for 'chemtrails' you will find hundreds of websites dedicated to a paranoid conspiracy theory that planes are spraying the atmosphere with climate-altering chemicals. Believers collect photographs of the spreading vapour trails from jets as 'proof' that the government/UN/corporations are spraying chemicals that, they claim, cause droughts, famine and disease. The irony here is that spreading jet vapour trails are indeed changing the climate. When planes were grounded across the US following the 9/11 attacks temperatures fell by 1°C (1.8°F). What is interesting is that people need a conspiracy and an enemy before they become energized by it.

Smokescreens

Marc Roberts has turned my 'rant' about smokers and climate change into a great one-page comic. Visit the 21 April 2007 posting on www.throbgoblins.blogspot.com.

Many people don't believe the odds I quote of a being hit by a meteorite. There is a handy list of relative odds at www.livescience.com/forcesofnature/050106_odds_of_ dying.html. To be strictly accurate, though, the odds I gave for the lottery are the odds of winning on any single ticket. The odds I gave of being killed by a meteorite are the odds during your entire life. It is also a different kind of risk – lotteries effect very few people with great regularity, whereas meteorites strike very rarely but with effects that are often catastrophic.

Stifling your inner sceptic

Not only have oil and coal companies adopted the tactics of the tobacco companies, but, as George Monbiot reveals in his book *Heat* (page 317), it was often the same public relations companies, front groups and scientists that crossed over from denying the danger of tobacco to denying the danger of climate change. George shows that one of the first front groups to attack the climate scientists, the

Advancement of Sound Science Coalition, was originally formed by Philip Morris tobacco to undermine the argument that sidestream smoke was dangerous to non-smokers. It only took up the issue of climate change because it needed to find a wider range of issues to look like a real research group.

The activities of the climate deniers have been very well documented – there is only a handful of them after all. Good sources are www.sourcewatch.org, the 'Hall of Shame' on www.risingtide.org.uk and www.theheatisonline.org. There is also an excellent website dedicated to uncovering the web of organizations and deniers funded by Exxon Mobil, www.exxonsecrets.org. For the low-down on Bjorn Lomborg visit www.anti-lomborg.com.

Bad messengers

For an interesting take on the lack of diversity in the green movement see an article by Van Jones, 'Is the Green Movement too White?' at www.commongroundmag.com/2007/04/eco-apartheid0704.html.

In July 2007 Ipsos MORI released a report called *Tipping Point or Turning Point* that summarized their polling research into public attitudes around climate change. MORI reported that when people were asked who they 'trusted to tell the truth' 72 per cent said scientists, 56 per cent said the 'ordinary person on the street' and only 20 per cent said politicians. Below all of them came journalists with 19 per cent. People were not asked about environmental campaigners, but trade union officials received 41 per cent. The same report revealed that only 21 per cent of people disagree with the statement that 'many leading experts still question if human activity is contributing to climate change'. Sadly, that inner sceptic is embedded in far too many people.

Steve Hounsham's analogy with *Dad's Army* is taken from *Painting the Town Green*. See www.green-engage. co.uk/project_painting.html.

For an excellent analysis of the denial of human rights abuses read *States of Denial* by Stanley Cohen (Polity Press). I have written an article that draws on Professor Cohen's work to make analogies with climate change at www. ecoglobe.ch/motivation/e/clim2922.htm.

The pick-and-mix stand
The starting point was a similar set set of excuses by Mayer Hillman in *How We can Save the Planet* (see page 318) on which I have expanded and elaborated.

Comedy corner
Don't believe me? Read the original article at www.telegraph.co.uk/news/main.jhtml?xml=/news/2007/ 03/17/noleary17.xml.

Climate change – bring it on!
The articles are 'Sydney told to expect deadly warming spike', Associated Press, 31 January 2007 and 'Vino Veritas', Lloyds List, 30 April 2004.

The plastic bag fetish
Here are the figures:
• The embodied emissions of a plastic bag is 6.25 kg ($13^3/_4$ lb) of CO_2 (equivalent) per kilogram of plastic. It is interesting that the embodied emissions of cotton are about the same.
• Each plastic bag weighs, on average, 5 g ($^1/_5$ oz). So each bag produces 0.0312 kg ($^1/_{10}$ lb) of CO_2.

In an article for the environmental magazine *Resurgence* (not available on the web) Oliver Tickell points out that the oil that goes into plastic bags 'represents only about 0.17 per cent of production. Put another way, only about 2½ minutes' worth of global oil production goes into plastic bags every day. Our use of plastic bags accounts for less than 43 seconds' worth of daily per capita waste production.

Hiding in the crowd
There is a detailed debunking of the frog in a pot myth at www.snopes.com/critters/wild/frogboil.asp.

There is a good description of the relationship between the bystander effect and the denial of human rights abuses in Stanley Cohen's excellent book *States of Denial* (see above).

Meet your Evil Carbon Twin
There is a list of 'evil twins' in popular culture at http://en.wikipedia.org/wiki/Evil_twin.

Regarding the threat of the Chinese tsunami, someone actually worked out the physics of all the Chinese people jumping at the same time. It would have the force of 500 tonnes of tnt, which would hardly cause a ripple. See www.straightdope.com/classics/a1_155.html.

Interestingly, a rogue conceptual artist, Torsten Lauschmann, used this mass jump concept to call on people to jump to prevent climate change. On his hoax website, www.worldjumpday.org, he calls on 600 million people to jump simultaneously in order to 'stop global warming, extend daytime hours and create a more homogenous climate'.

Part 5: Strategies for dealing with climate change

Adapt

The predictions of future flooding risk are taken from the Foresight Report of the UK flood and Coastal Defence Project. You can find the report and a handy executive summary at www.foresight.gov.uk/previous_projects/flood_ and_coastal_defence/index.html.

This report makes chilling reading because it is clear that the potential risks are very high indeed. The wide range in the forecasts suggests to me that the government has no real idea of what the actual risks are.

The UK Environment Agency has spent £3million on a national flood risk map. You can visit it and find the flood risk to your own street at www.environment-agency.gov.uk/subjects/flood/?lang=_e.

The dark blue areas on the map show the streets that currently have a 1 per cent or more chance of flooding (once in a hundred years) and the light blue areas show the streets that have of a 0.1 per cent chance (once in a thousand years). Of course, these odds will shorten dramatically with increasing climate change.

Regarding Spain, read the article 'Spain is New "Poster Child" of Climate Impacts' at www.heatisonline.org/contentserver/objecthandlers/index.cfm?id=6259&method=full and 'Pain in Spain: Lesson for All' at www.inunis.net/assets/downloads/Pain_in_Spain_10%20eb07.pdf.

The University of Oxford report I quote is 'The 40% House'. It can be downloaded at http://www.eci.ox.ac.uk/research/energy/40house.php.

Part 7: Preparing for the detox

The thinking in this chapter draws on the substantial body of research into behaviour change. Three of the best reports are: 'Personal Responsibility and Changing Behaviour' from the Prime Minister's Strategy Unit at www.strategy-unit. gov.uk. 'Carrots, Sticks and Sermons' by Demos/ Green Alliance atwww.demos.co.uk/publications/carrrots-stickssermons.

'Motivating Sustainable Consumption' by the Sustainable Development Research Network at www.sd-research. org.uk/publications.php.

Say no to sackcloth

For a good sense of the awful stifling clutter of the middle-class Victorian home read *The Victorian House* by Judith Flanders (HarperPerennial).

Buying great stuff

Good places to look for low-energy green gadgets are
The 'Green Shop' at www.cat.org
www.greenshop.co.uk
www.ecoutlet.co.uk
www.gonegreen.co.uk
www.naturalcollection.com

Biofuels

You can refit your car or van to run on vegetable oil using the kit supplied by vegetec. We meet the vegetec executive director, Mike Lawton, in the Thrivers chapter.

There is a list of biofuel suppliers at www.biodieselfill-ingstations.co.uk, although you will need to ask the individual suppliers if they are using waste cooking oil. You need to be wary of get-rich-quick merchants selling substandard fuel. Jon Halle of www.goldenfuels.org has told me of a simple test you can perform to check the quality. Jon advises that if a vendor refuses to let you do this test then don't think of buying from him.

'Put a small quantity of water in a jam jar and add the same amount of biodiesel. Close the lid tightly and give the jar ten good shakes. Then put it down to settle. Pure biodiesel and water don't mix, so within a minute or two of shaking good fuel it should separate and float on more-or-less clear water. Badly made biodiesel will often have been poorly washed or purified and contains soaps. The layers will take much longer to separate and the water will remain cloudy, possibly with a layer of white soap between them.'

Part 8: Counting the carbos

There are also many web-based carbon calculators, which are reviewed at www.coinet.org.uk/solutions/carbon calculations.

Land transport

My observation is that people rarely know how many miles they commute by public transport, but they know very well how much time they spend doing it. The estimates for each hour spent travelling are derived from the average distance covered by different forms of public transport in an hour multiplied by their emissions for distance. I then multiplied this by 48 weeks – I am assuming a month annual holiday.

It is worth noting that people can run up more emissions in an hour's train commute than in an hour's car commute during rush hour because they can cover far more distance in the same time.

Similarly, the reason that a city bus has lower emissions

than an inter-city bus is that it travels far less distance in an hour.

You can find the emissions per mile or km of all new cars at www.vcacarfueldata.org.uk.

Flights and boats

'Predict and Decide: Aviation, Climate Change and UK Policy' is a very good overview of the issues with flying and their implications for UK emissions reductions. See www.eci. ox.ac.uk/research/energy/predictanddecide.php.

The IPCC has produced an overview of the science on the impacts of flying at http://www.grida.no/climate/ipcc/aviation/. However, this is very dense and there is a good summary in chapter two of 'Predict and Decide' (see above).

The figures on boats are based on my own calculations taking figures from Cunard and with additional data from Best Foot Forward (www.bestfootforward.com).

For a sense of the potential for ships to reduce their energy use see http://environment.newscientist.com/channel/earth/energy-fuels/mg18524881.600.

Food

I am indebted to Laurie Michaelis of the Quaker Living Witness project, and this food calculator is derived from the inspired carbon calculator he wrote for Quaker Green Action, which you can download at www.living-witness.org.uk/home_files/Personal%20GHG%20 calculator.pdf.

Laurie used to work on emissions research for the Organization for Economic Cooperation and Development (OECD) and has done the best work I know on pulling apart the data on agriculture impacts using statistics from DEFRA, the UN Food and Agriculture Organization and the national greenhouse gas inventory statistics.

What you buy

This is a complex area, but I was still surprised to find very little work on calculating emissions from the goods and services we buy. Most calculators ignore this area altogether even though this is one the largest sources of emissions to fall within the control of the individual, so I realized that I would have to develop a calculator myself.

I started with the UK Household Expenditure study of the Statistics Office, which provides a detailed breakdown of UK household spending by category. I matched the categories of household expenditure that had not already been measured in the carbo-counter – worth some £332 billion – against the total UK emissions from the goods and services sector. This was adjusted and weighted according to the household expenditure categories into high, standard or low emissions spending.

The multiplier of one for manufactured good is approximated from a range of embedded emissions statistics but seems to work well enough. A laptop computer, for example, costs up to a £1,000 and has emissions of around a tonne of carbon dioxide equivalent. The multiplier of 0.1 for low-carbon spending is approximate and based on a few enquiries that revealed that heating and electric expenditure for charity shops was around 2–5 per cent of turnover, which approximate to around 0.2 carbos per £1. And of course many labour-based services have virtually no emissions.

This calculator assumes that the emissions of imported goods and services are equal to those of exported goods and services. Given that much manufacturing and heavy energy-intensive industry has shifted to the Far East there is a possibility that it is underestimating emissions – after all, the huge increase in Chinese emissions has been fuelled by production for export. However, things are never that simple – much of the UK's exports are in the investment and financial services sector, which are helping to fund economic growth elsewhere. This is a rule of thumb but it seems to work well enough.

Finally, for a good discussion of the issues with offsetting see the report 'The Carbon Neutral Myth: Offset Indulgences for Your Climate Sins' at www.carbon-tradewatch.org/ pubs/carbon_neutral_myth.pdf.

Part 9: Drop a tonne

This book is designed as a first step to get you on the way to a lighter detoxed life. I have therefore been careful to provide broad pointers towards the areas where you can make that change rather than provide a point-by-point manual about how to do it.

There are many places to get more information on how to reduce your emissions in each of these categories. In addition to the books on pages 316–19, a good starting point can be found at www.direct.gov.uk/en/ Environmentandgreenerliving, which provides detailed advice for all aspects covered in the Drop a Tonne section.

You can read former articles from the *Ecologist* on all the aspects of green living at www.theecologist.co.uk/ daily_life.asp. I have also built a list of contacts for each of these sections at www.carbondetox.org.

Your totals

The overall UK emissions figures were taken from the official government emissions statistics for 2005 at

www.defra.gov.uk/environment/statistics/globatmos/kf/
gakf07.htm and averaged across the UK population to give
the carbos for the average UK person. The proportions of
emissions for different activities were taken from the
Department of Trade and Industry Energy statistics, see
http://stats.berr.gov.uk/energystats/dukes07.pdf. There are
no official statistics for the emissions from the flights of UK
citizens so I had to construct my own estimate using
European Union aviation statistics and UK airport passenger
statistics.

Drop a tonne at home

First of all you can be inspired by the knowledge that other
people have taken standard houses and cut their emissions
by a half to two-thirds. You can get a load of ideas and an
understanding of the theory at www.theyellowhouse.org.uk
(yes I admit, it's my own house). Twenty people have
written up their own eco-renovation experiences at
www.ecovation.org.uk.

For insulation schemes contact your local Energy Advice
Centres. They all have the same phone number, which
magically switches you to your local branch: 0800 512 012.

Reputable suppliers of solar panels are all members of the
solar trade association. See www.solartradeassociation.
org.uk. I would strongly recommend that you refuse to work
with any installer who is not a member.

You can find information on grants and ideas on wood
burners at www.lowcarbonbuildings.org.uk.

There is a guide to renewable energy suppliers and tariffs at
www.gooshing.co.uk/home_energy and www.energywatch.
org.uk/greentariff.pdf.

There is a good report on the 'greenness' of renewable
energy suppliers at www.ncc.org.uk/responsibleconsumption/

green-tariffs.pdf.

For the DIY weekenders I strongly recommend *The Eco-house Manual* by Nigel Griffiths (page 318).

Regarding the old chestnut about the relative merits of hand dishwashing versus dishwashers visit www.landtechnik. unibonn.de/ifl_research/ht_1/EEDAL_03_ManualDishwa shing.pdf. Never before (and I hope never again) has the issue been visited so exhaustively.

Drop a tonne on land travel

There are car-sharing sites at www.carshare.com, www.nationalcarshare.co.uk, www.shareacar.com and www.liftshare.org. I can't vouch for any of them.

If you want to buy a new more efficient car, check the emissions at www.vcacarfueldata.org.uk.

Yes it really does cost that much to run a car. See http://money.guardian.co.uk/news_/story/0,,1927402,00. html.

Drop a tonne on air travel

If you want to take the train in Europe instead of flying, your first point of call should be www.seat61.com, which will tell you everything you need to know about the routes, times and booking requirement of trains. To get good prices, trains need to be booked long in advance, so always plan ahead.

For a very personal take on the challenges posed by reducing flying see http://casaubonsbook.blogspot.com/ 2007/02/love-miles.html.

And, if you feel strongly, you can add you name to the people who pledge never to fly again at www.flightpledge. org.uk/.

Drop a tonne on food

The *Ecologist* has a list of organic box suppliers at www.theecologist.co.uk/banner.asp?banner_id=4.

There is an online directory of organic shops, farms and suppliers at www.whyorganic.org/involved_organicDirectory.asp.

Drop a tonne on stuff

For second-hand buying there is the huge www.ebay.co.uk site. There is also an ever-growing network of membership networks in which people simply give things away to each other. See www.uk.freecycle.org for details of your local groups.

Part 10: Thriving

You can find out more about the work of our thrivers at:

Penney Poyzer – www.msarch.co.uk/ecohome

Mike Lawton – www.regenatec.com/

Paul Bodenham – www.operationnoah.org/

Antony Turner – www.carbonsense.org

Part 11: Taking control

This is such a rapidly moving field that I have decided to point you towards the carbon detox website www.carbondetox where I provide up-to-date ideas and direction.

Index

Acknowledgements

I have been hugely privileged to have had the support, ideas and feedback of some of the most creative people working on climate change and social change.

First of all, a big hoorah to Dave Hampton (www.carbon-coach.org) who started this project rolling and came up with the title Carbon Detox, Mark Lynas who persuaded me to do it, and Sandra Rigby and Clare Churly at Gaia who have steered it to completion.

A special thanks must go to the review team who read and commented extensively on the draft manuscript: Alastair Macintosh, Annie Levy, Chris Goodall, Dorothy Cowie, Craig Simmonds, George Monbiot, Graham Anderson, Hugh Warwick, Kezia Rolfe, Jo Hamilton, Laurie Michaelis, Mark Lynas, Matt Sellwood, Mayer Hillman, Mim Saxl, Nicola Baird, Patrick Anderson, Pete Austin, Roman Krznaric and Zoe Warwick.

They identified all the places where I was boring, confusing, offensive or wrong. Just think how awful this book was before they were let loose on it.

Thanks to Andrew Simms, Caspar Henderson, Chris Rose, Ed Gillespie, James Lockhart, Jon Halle, Matt Prescott, Dr. Mike Sparrow and Oliver Tickell for information and advice on particular aspects of this book.

Thanks to the 'Thrivers' for their time and inspiration: Antony Turner, Mike Lawton, Paul Bodenham, Pauline Lazoya and Penney Poyzer.

This book was written in the Greens Café on St Giles, Oxford and researched using their free wi-fi. Hopefully the first of many books to come from this delightful little café.

And finally, a huge thanks to Annie for her love and support and to Tim Baster and Cliff Jordan whose confident leadership at COIN freed me up to complete this book against a very tight deadline.

I just hope you don't all expect a free copy.